Cambridge Elements

Elements in Ancient East Asia
IDEAS: Religion and Philosophy, and the Arts and Sciences
edited by
Erica Fox Brindley
Pennsylvania State University
Rowan Kimon Flad
Harvard University

SELF AND BODY IN EARLY EAST ASIAN THOUGHT

Mark Edward Lewis
Stanford University

CAMBRIDGE
UNIVERSITY PRESS

Shaftesbury Road, Cambridge CB2 8EA, United Kingdom

One Liberty Plaza, 20th Floor, New York, NY 10006, USA

477 Williamstown Road, Port Melbourne, VIC 3207, Australia

314–321, 3rd Floor, Plot 3, Splendor Forum, Jasola District Centre, New Delhi – 110025, India

103 Penang Road, #05–06/07, Visioncrest Commercial, Singapore 238467

Cambridge University Press is part of Cambridge University Press & Assessment, a department of the University of Cambridge.

We share the University's mission to contribute to society through the pursuit of education, learning and research at the highest international levels of excellence.

www.cambridge.org
Information on this title: www.cambridge.org/9781009486897

DOI: 10.1017/9781108975803

When citing this work, please include a reference to the DOI 10.1017/9781108975803

First published 2024

A catalogue record for this publication is available from the British Library

ISBN 978-1-009-48689-7 Hardback
ISBN 978-1-108-97219-2 Paperback
ISSN 2632-7325 (online)
ISSN 2632-7317 (print)

Self and Body in Early East Asian Thought

Elements in Ancient East Asia

DOI: 10.1017/9781108975803
First published online: December 2024

Mark Edward Lewis
Stanford University

Author for correspondence: Mark Edward Lewis, mel1000@standford.edu

Abstract: This Element examines evolving methods of cultivating the embodied self, including healing diseases and creating a superior person, in late Warring States and early imperial East Asia. It analyses many topics, including the textualization of bodily regimens and therapies, their systematization, their dissemination among different (and sometimes rival) social groups, and the diversity of traditions – religious, pharmacological, nourishing of life – that contested and combined to form a hegemonic medical practice. These topics in turn feature several issues: models of the body, regimens of cultivating and extending vitality, models of disease, and therapies for these ailments. All these ideas will be refined and extended through comparison with early Western medical traditions.

Keywords: self, body, nourishing, healing, physicians

ISBNs: 9781009486897 (HB), 9781108972192 (PB), 9781108975803 (OC)
ISSNs: 2632-7325 (online), 2632-7317 (print)

Contents

Introduction

While the "self" and "body" seem immediately perceptible and comprehensible in their physicality, they are largely cultural constructs which change over time and space, thus requiring historical study. Their modern academic study began with classic essays by Marcel Mauss in the mid-1930s.[1] The essay on the "category of the person/self" argued that this was at its simplest a universal category, as indicated by the possibility in all languages of referring to a self which was distinguished from others. At the next level, the self could be theorized as defined roles, obligations and rights pertaining to those roles, and an ethical character that together defined the nature of a person (*personne*), and which varied among cultures. The article also suggested (without always clearly distinguishing) an interiorized self (*moi*) defined by psychological states, relations to the cosmos, and spiritual relations to other such selves.[2] Finally, it sketched a triumphalist account of the emergence of a unique Western theory of the person as first a philosophical-religious conception (articulated in Christianity's theory of the soul), and ultimately a fundamental intellectual category (in modern thinking from Descartes's *cogito* through Kant) underlying the emergence of an individualism that treated the self as a discreet monad existing wholly within the mind and detached from the body (Ryle's "ghost in a machine"). This understanding was foundational to the modern world.[3]

[1] "Une Catégorie de l'esprit humain: La Notion de personne, celle de 'moi'," (1935) and "Les Techniques du corps," (1934) are both in the classic one-volume collection of his major essays, Mauss Marcel, *Sociologie et anthropologie*, ed. Claude Lévi-Strauss (Paris: Presses Universitaires de France, 1950), pp. 331–386. A translation of the essay on the person/self, along with essays on its theoretical significance and case studies are published in Michael Carrithers, Steven Collins, and Steven Lukes, eds., *The Category of the Person: Anthropology, Philosophy, History* (Cambridge: Cambridge University Press, 1985). This volume, pp. 302–303, lists recent (prior to 1985) major studies on the person/self.

[2] See also Richard Sorabji, *Self: Ancient and Modern Insights about Individuality, Life, and Death* (Chicago: University of Chicago Press, 2006); Charles Larmore, *Les Pratiques du moi* (Paris: Presses Universitaires de France, 2004); Hermann Schmitz, *Selbst sein: Über Identität, Subjektivität und Personalität* (Munich: Verlag Karl Alber, 2013). This last elaborates theories of an interior self, a "person" that straddles the inner self and the outer world of roles and rights, and a body that is crucial to understanding both. See also Schmitz, *Zur Epigenese der Person* (Munich: Verlag Karl Alber, 2017).

[3] Versions of a theory of the self that is fundamental to individualism and to modernity are elaborated in Charles Taylor, *Sources of the Self: The Making of Modern Identity* (Cambridge: Cambridge University Press, 1989); Larry Siedentop, *Inventing the Individual: The Origins of Western Liberalism* (Cambridge, Mass.: Harvard University Press, 2014); Gerald N. Izenberg, *Impossible Individuality: Romanticism, Revolution, and the Origins of Modern Selfhood, 1787–1802* (Princeton: Princeton University Press, 1992); Jerrold Seigel, *The Idea of the Self: Thought and Experience in Western Europe since the Seventeenth Century* (Cambridge: Cambridge University Press, 2005); John O. Lyons, *The Invention of the Self: The Hinge of Consciousness in the Eighteenth Century* (Carbondale: Southern Illinois University Press, 1978); Karl Joachim Weintraub, *The Value of the Individual: Self and Circumstance in Autobiography* (Chicago: University of Chicago Press, 1978).

Several critical essays and case studies written to accompany the English translation of the essay trace the crucial initial step to the philosophy of Plato rather than Christianity. Others reject this evolutionary perspective, arguing instead that the diverse practices and theories that guided both the psychologically defined inner "self" (*moi*) and the exterior "person" (*personne*) shaped by rules and laws should be treated as episodes moving toward no clear conclusion. This latter position underlies the writing over the decades of numerous studies on the theory and practice of the "person" in diverse cultures, a discourse within which this work is situated.

Mauss's essay on "techniques of the body" (written a year earlier and influenced by Marcel Granet's discussions of "bodily techniques" in early China) argued that each society developed distinctive techniques for training the body, techniques which shaped both physical capacities and associated mental mechanisms adapted to their visions of social order. Thus, the body of the Greek citizen trained for the public agon was distinct from that of a monk in his cell, or that of a modern citizen alternating between a home and the site of paid labor. Whereas the purely physical and measurable body of modern science had no history, Mauss's body conceived through its "modes of construction" was "thoroughly historicized and completely problematic."[4]

This model allowed the body to be approached from numerous disciplines – history, anthropology, philosophy, sociology, art history, religion – and a vast array of perspectives. The three-volume collection *Fragments for a History of the Human Body* divided these perspectives under three rubrics. First, some employed a "vertical axis," examining training of the body to facilitate its relation to divinities above or animals below. The former included exercises through which one approached a god spatially or came to resemble one physically, training to modify those features that prevented people from participating in the divine, or rites of healing through pilgrimage or exorcism.[5] For the latter,

---

Michel Foucault's oeuvre focuses on the creation of the modern individual, but argues that the institutions and norms that created this person – the medical clinic, asylum, prison, and sexuality – did so through confinement and carceral discipline. See also Anthony Elliott, *Concepts of the Self* (Cambridge: Polity, 2001).

4 See Michel Feher, Ramona Naddaff, and Nadia Tazi, eds., *Fragments for a History of the Human Body*, 3 vols. (New York: Zone, 1989), "Introduction" (by Michel Feher), p. 11. These volumes provide a useful sketch of the many approaches to the body at that time. For reviews of the impact of this bodily focus on history and anthropology, see Carolyn Walker Bynum, "Why All the Fuss about the Body? A Medievalist's Perspective," *Critical Inquiry* 22 (Autumn, 1995), pp. 1–33; Thomas J. Csordas, "Embodiment and Cultural Phenomenology," in *Perspectives on Embodiment*, ed. Gail Weiss and Honi Haber (New York: Routledge, 1999), pp. 143–162; Csordas, "Introduction: The Body as Representation and Being-in-the-World," in *Embodiment and Experience: The Existential Ground of Culture and Self* (Cambridge: Cambridge University Press, 1994), pp. 1–24; Justin E. H. Smith, ed., *Embodiment: A History* (Oxford: Oxford University Press, 2017).

5 Csordas, *The Sacred Self: A Cultural Phenomenology of Charismatic Healing* (Berkeley: University of California Press, 1994); *Body/Meaning/Healing* (Basingstoke: Palgrave MacMillan, 2002); Judith Perkins, *The Suffering Self: Pain and Narrative Representation in*

one developed aspects of the body that distinguished human beings from animals, or alternatively (as in the "Chart on Guiding and Pulling" [*dao yin tu* 導引徒] from Mawangdui that will be discussed later) imitated animals whose powers could extend human capacities. The second axis was "horizontal," primarily the relations of "inside" and "outside," often cultivating a soul or intelligence hidden within, or modulating the emotions, desires, and other sensations that emerged from the interior. The final rubric was "the classical distinction between organ and function," which included using bodily organs or substances as metaphors for aspects of human society, or cultivating attributes that embodied the status or role of honored types.

The most wide-ranging study of theories of the person, self, and body in early in China is Lisa Raphals, *A Tripartite Self: Body, Mind and Spirit in Early China*.[6] This book surveys most early Chinese discussions of these topics, and presents the key modern studies. Its most important argument is to elaborate the contrast between philosophical texts, which tend to emphasize the heart-mind's mastery over the body, and the texts on self-cultivation or medical treatment of the body which emphasize the key importance of the self's substances (most importantly *qi* energies) and its "spirit" (*shen* 神, also translated "soul"). The former tends to produce dualistic models that oppose mind and body, while the latter produce the "tripartite self" (of the title), elaborating a corporeal view in which both body and mind consist of such vital substances as (in order of increasing refinement) *qi*, "essence" (*jing* 精), and spirit. The discussions in this book overlap with many of the texts studied here, so it deserves careful reading.

However, the single most useful elaboration of the interlinked ideas of self, person, and body in early China is probably David Hall and Roger Ames's model of the "focus-field self," which is expounded in several books and essays.[7]

the Early Christian Era (London: Routledge, 1995); Zsuzsanna Várhelyi, "Self-Care and Health-Care: Selfhood and Religion in the Roman Imperial Elite," in *Religious Dimensions of the Self in the Second Century CE*, ed. Jörg Rüpke and Greg Woolf (Tübingen: Mohr Siebeck, 2013), pp. 221–242; Byron J. Good, *Medicine, Rationality, and Experience: An Anthropological Perspective* (Cambridge: Cambridge University Press, 1994), ch. 5; Bruce Kapferer, *A Celebration of Demons: Exorcism and the Aesthetics of Healing in Sri Lanka* (Washington, DC: Berg, 1983); Robert A. Scott, *Miracle Cures: Saints, Pilgrimages, and the Healing Powers of Belief* (Berkeley: University of California Press, 2010); Ruth Harris, *Lourdes: Body and Spirit in the Secular Age* (London: Penguin, 1999); Élisabeth Claverie, *Les Guerres de la Vierge: Une anthropologie des apparitions* (Paris: Gallimard, 2003).

[6] Raphals, *Tripartite Self* (Oxford: Oxford University Press, 2023). On the emergence of soul-body dualism, see also Edward Slingerland, *Mind and Body in Early China: Beyond Orientalism and the Myth of Holism* (Oxford: Oxford University Press, 2019). On the pivotal role of philosophy in the evolving ideas about the body and self, see Zhang Zailin 張再林, *Zuowei shenti zhexue de zhongguo gudai zhexue* 作為身體哲學的中國古代哲學 (Beijing: Zhonguo Shehui Kexue Chubanshe, 2008).

[7] David Hall and Ames, *Thinking through Confucius* (Albany: SUNY Press, 1987), pp. 125, 153, 192, 237–247; Ames, "The Focus-Field Self in Classical Confucianism," in *Self as Person in*

This theory is particularly valuable in that it not only offers insights into the full range of early Chinese ideas, but also (as I will discuss below) facilitates fruitful dialogue with some of the most important Western ideas about the relation of the self and the body. The idea of the "focus-field self" – which Ames elaborates primarily through Confucian and Daoist thinkers – views the person as a "focused" center embedded within an encompassing "field," or rather fields, consisting of other people, places, and, ultimately, the cosmos. This person is defined by a range of roles which he or she enacts relationally with others: son of a father or mother, elder brother of a younger brother, a descendant of deceased ancestors, etc. The person defined by these roles, obligations, and rights (to cite the Maussian idea) exists only within and through these multiple relations, not only those to close kin, but in weakening fashion with more distant kin, fellow villagers, the state's agents, and nonhumans. As emphasized more in the Daoist thinkers, any person also exists relationally as the focus of multiple fields formed with the creatures and objects within his or her ambit, and at the highest level with the cosmos viewed with the self as center. Likewise, things in the world can be understood through the multiple fields of which they form the focus/center, for example, the capital within the state, the court within the capital, the ruler within the court, etc. In all these fields radiating outward around a focus/center there is no absolute boundary between the selves and their "outside," a fact that is as true of the body as of the person.[8]

Asian Theory and Practice, ed. Roger T. Ames, Wimal Dissanayake, and Thomas P. Kasulis (Albany: SUNY Press, 1994), pp. 187–212; Hall and Ames, *Anticipating China: Thinking through the Narratives of Chinese and Western Culture* (Albany: SUNY Press, 1995), pp. 234–244, 268–278; *Thinking from the Han: Self, Truth, and Transcendence in Chinese and Western Culture* (Albany: SUNY Press, 1998), pp. 23–78; Ames, *Confucian Role Ethics: A Vocabulary* (Honolulu: University of Hawai'i Press, 2011), pp. 66–79; Ames, *Human Becomings: Theorizing Persons for Confucian Role Ethics* (Albany: SUNY Press, 2021), ch. 4. See also Thomas Kasulis, Ames, and Wimal Dissanayake, *Self as Body in Asian Theory and Practice* (Albany: SUNY Press, 1993), part 3; Ames and Dissanayake, eds., *Self and Deception: A Cross-Cultural Philosophical Enquiry* (Albany: SUNY Press, 1996); Ames, Kasulis, and Wissanayke, eds., *Self as Image in Asian Theory and Practice* (Albany: SUNY Press, 1998). For an overview of theories about early Chinese ideas of the self and the body, see Alexus McLeod, *The Dao of Madness: Mental Illness and Self-Cultivation in Early Chinese Philosophy and Medicine* (Oxford: Oxford University Press, 2021), ch. 1. On other aspects of "inner-outer" and the body, see Raphals, *Tripartite Self*, pp. 49–51, 208–215; Constance A. Cook, *Medicine and Healing Ancient East Asia: View from Excavated Texts*, Cambridge Elements in Ancient East Asia (Cambridge: Cambridge University Press, 2023), pp. 16–18.

8 Deborah Sommer, "Boundaries of the *Ti* Body," *Asia Major* 21.1(2008): 293–324; Sommer, "The Ji Self in Early Chinese Texts," in *Selfhood East and West: De-constructions of Identity*, ed. Jason Dockstader, Hans-Georg Moller, and Gunter Wohlfahrt (Traugott Bautz, 2012), pp. 17–45; Nathan Sivin, "State, Cosmos, and Body in the Last Three Centuries B.C." *Harvard Journal of Asiatic Studies* 55.1 (1995): 5–37; He Jianjin, "The Body in the Politics and Society of Early China," Ph.D. dissertation, University of Oregon, 2007; N. Scheper-Hughes and M. M. Lock, "The Mindful Body: A Prolegomenon to Future Work in Medical Anthropology," *Medical Anthropology Quarterly* 1 (1987): 6–41; Yang Rubin 楊儒賓, *Rujia shenti guan* 儒家身體觀

While the Ames/Hall model emphasizes the multiple and evolving relations within which the person emerges, Chinese thought elaborated a similar image through the idea of *qi* (氣), translated as "energy," "vital breath," "pneuma," or "vapor." This protean concept remains central to Chinese medicine, martial arts, strategy, calligraphy, and any form of dynamism. In the centuries covered in this essay it named a primal "stuff" or "configured energy" that constituted all entities, being common to inanimate matter, plants, animals, and people. This shared substrate meant that not only people and their environment shared common principles, but also that they acted directly upon one another through their *qi*, which thus provided a physical underpinning to the focus-field model. Consequently, the outer world could drive the feelings and actions of the embodied self, and that self could radiate outward to control other humans, and even aspects of the physical world.

The earliest known graphic form of the word *qi* appears in fourth century BCE bamboo strips found in Chu tombs. The graph consists of a phonetic element over one of two semantic signifiers indicating either "fire" or "heart," suggesting dynamism associated with the mind or spirit. The Qin tended to confuse this graph with one indicating "a gift of food," an in the Han it was commonly written with "cloud" or "vapor" over "grain." Thus, by the late Warring States people seem to have associated it with the vapors rising from cooked grain. However, it was most closely linked to the idea of wind, which provided a model for its actions and served as a gloss or in synonym compounds. It was the substance of the desires and emotions that drove human actions, and in its more refined forms it also became the "essence" (*jing*) and "spirit" (*shen*) that were essential to human cogitation, reproduction, and interaction with spirits. It provided a central concept in philosophy, early healing arts, and textually constituted technical medicine for analyzing the construction both of the person and the body, and indeed for the overlapping of these two to form an embodied self.[9]

(Taipei: Zhonyang yanjiuyuan Zhonguo wen zhe yanjiusuo chou bei chu 中央研究院中國文哲研究手籌備處, 1999).

9 Cook, *Medicine and Healing in Ancient East Asia*, pp. 14–16; Mark Edward Lewis, *Sanctioned Violence in Early China* (Albany: SUNY Press, 1990), ch. 6; Shigehisa Kuriyama, "The Imagination of Winds and the Development of the Chinese Conception of the Body," in *Body, Subject & Power in China*, ed. Angela Zito and Tani Barlow (Chicago: University of Chicago Press, 1994), pp. 23–41, esp. 34–38; Kuriyama, *The Expressiveness of the Body and the Divergence of Greek and Chinese Medicine* (New York: Zone, 1999), ch. 6, "Wind and Self"; Michael Stanley-Baker, "*Qi* 氣: A Means for Cohering Natural Knowledge," in *Routledge Handbook of Chinese Medicine*, ed. Vivienne Lo and Michael Stanley-Baker, with Dolly Yang (London: Routledge, 2022), pp. 23–50. On glossing *qi* as "vapor," and its use in early medical literature, see Donald Harper, *Early Chinese Medical Literature: The Mawangdui Medical Manuscripts* (London: Kegan Paul, 1998), pp. 5–6, 24–25, 69–93, 118–139, 143–147, 163–166, 173–179. For the gloss as "configured energy," see Manfred Porkert, *The Theoretical Foundations of Chinese Medicine: Systems of Correspondence* (Cambridge, Mass.: The MIT Press, 1974), pp. 62, 168–176. See also Yang Rubin, ed., *Zhongguo gudai sixiang shi Zhong de qi lun yu shenti guan* 中國古代史中的氣論與身體觀 (Taipei: Juliu Tushu Gongsi, 1993); Cai

With its permeable boundaries, mutual interactions, and interpenetration of bodily substances and mental processes, this "focus-field" person created by the movements of *qi* has been presented as distinctively Chinese, opposed to a Western self, defined by the radical separation of mind and body, and the clear definition of the measurable, physical body. However, this must be qualified. First, numerous German scholars have endorsed the *qi*-based model as a superior approach to the human body.[10] This is in part explained by the fact that the German language distinguishes the Latin-derived *Körper*, which indicates the measurable physical body or the corpse, from *Leib*, the subjective body of feelings, sensations, perceptions, and emotions, or broadly the person's temperament. As an example of this distinction, *Leibspeise* indicates one's favorite food. *Leib* matches well with the idea of a body defined through *qi* energies that link mental phenomena, physical organs, and surroundings.[11]

This has inspired phenomenologists to develop theories of a person constructed through the dynamism of the lived body, the back-and-forth between stimuli and responsive emotions, and the shaping impact of exterior "atmospheres." Most important is Hermann Schmitz, whose "new phenomenology" produced a ten-volume study moving from immediate bodily experience, through the energetic interchanges between body and environment, to the construction of multiple spaces for such cultural phenomena as art, law, and the divine. His model of the body frequently appeals to the Homeric world, where people experienced emotions as invading, external powers, and which were distributed through many sites within the body (rather than confined within the mind). The model, and related theories of objective external "atmospheres" created by crowd sentiments, the

Fanglu 蔡方鹿, *Qi* 氣 (Beijing: Zhongguo Renmin Daxue Chubanshe, 1990), ch. 1–2; Chen Dexing 陳德興, *Qi lun shi wu de shenti zhexue: Yinyang, wuxing, jingqi lilun de shenti xinggou* 氣論釋物的身體哲學:陰陽,五行,景氣理論的身體形構 (Taipei: Wunan Tushu Chuban, 2009); Li Cunshan 李存山, *Qi lun yu ren xue* 氣論與仁學 (Zhengzhou: Zhongzhou Guji Chubanshe, 2009); Kuroda Genji 黑田源次, *Ki no kenkyū* 氣の研究 (Tokyo: Tokyo Bijutsu, 1977), book 1; Miura Kunio 三浦國雄, *Ki no Chūgoku bunka: Kikō, yōjō, fūsui, eki* 氣の中國文化:氣功, 養生, 風水, 易 (Osaka: Sōgensha, 1994). On "spirit" (shen) and the body, see Catherine Despeux, "Âmes et animation du corps: La notion de shen dans la médicine chinoise antique, " *Extrême-Orient Extrême Occident* 29 (2007): 71–94.

10 Gudula Linck, *Leib oder Körper: Mcnsch, Welt und Leben in der chineschischen Philosophie* (Munich: Verlag Karl Alber, 2012); Dominique Hertzer, *Das Leuchten des Geistes und die Erkenntnis der Seele: Die medizinische Vorstellung vom Seelischen als Ausdruck philosophischen Denkens – China und das Abendland* (VAS: Bad Homburg, 2006); Manfred Kubny, *Qi Lebenskraftkonzepte in China: Definitionen, Theorien und Grundlagen* (Heidelberg: Haug Verlag, 1995). On the use of early Chinese ideas about the lived body (or the body formed through living) in the thought of Martin Heidegger, see Thomas Michael, *Philosophical Enactment and Bodily Cultivation in Early Daoism: In the Matrix of the Daodejing* (London: Bloomsbury Academic, 2022), ch. 9.

11 Thomas Ots uses the German term *Leib* to explicate Chinese *qi gong* and certain medical practices. See "The Silenced Body – the Expressive *Leib*: On the Dialectic of Mind and Life in Chinese Cathartic Healing," in *Embodiment and Experience*, pp. 116–138.

moods produced by seasons or times of day, and the emotional impacts of architectural spaces, has all aroused interest in the idea of *qi* with its interchange between body, mind, and environment. Thus, the Chinese ideas facilitate Western theorizations of the person, the body, and health as being simultaneously physical, mental, and social phenomena.[12]

A second development in modern Western thought supporting study of the Chinese models are theories from the cognitive sciences that deny the mind's separation from the body, or the idea that reason can be independent of perception, movement, and ambient moods. Such writers argue that thinking is done with the body (or, in the case of spiders, with the web) as much as with the mind. Theories of "body thinking" again reject the mythicizing view of Chinese ideas as produced by a great "other," instead bringing theories of the embodied self in both traditions into dialogue.[13]

---

[12] In Schmitz's "System der Philosophie," see *Der Leib* (Bonn: Bouvier, 1965); *Der Leib im Spiegel der Kunst* (Bonn: Bouvier, 1966); *Der leibliche Raum* (Bonn: Bouvier, 1967); *Der Gefühlsraum* (Bonn: Bouvier, 1969); and *Die Person* (Bonn: Bouvier, 1980). See also *Leib und Gefühl*, 3rd ed. (Bielefeld: Sirius, 2008), *Atmosphären* (Munich: Verlag Karl Alber, 2016); and (on the origins in the West of the radical division between "objective" things and "subjective" states of mind) *Der Urspring des Gegenstandes: Von Parmenides bis Demokrit* (Bonn: Bouvier, 1988). For related theories of the body and surrounding "atmospheres," see Gernot Böhme, *Leib: Die Natur die wir selbst sind* (Berlin: Suhrkamp Verlag, 2019) (throughout Book 1 he elaborates his theory of the dynamic body and how it differs from Schmitz's); *Ethik leiblicher Existenz* (Berlin: Suhrkamp Verlage, 2008); *Leibsein als Aufgabe: Leibphilosophie in pragmatischer Hinsicht* (Kusterdingen: Graue Edition, 2003); *Atmosphäre: Essays zur neuen Ästhetik*, 4th ed. (Berlin: Suhrkamp Verlag, 2019); *Architektur und Atmosphäre*, 2nd ed. (Munich: Wilhelm Fink Verlag, 2013); *The Aesthetics of Atmospheres*, ed. Jean-Paul Thibaud (London: Routledge, 2017); Tonino Griffero, *Atmospheres: Aesthetics of Emotional Spaces*, tr. Sarah de Sanctis (London: Routledge, 2010). See also Hans-Georg Gadamer, *Über die Verborgenheit der Gesundheit* (Frankfurt am Main: Suhrkamp Verlag, 1993); Jackie Pigeaud, *La Maladie de l'âme: Étude sur la relation de l'âme et du corps dans la tradition médico-philosophique antique* (Paris: Les Belles Lettres, 2006). A similar overall argument, working from the body through the emotions to the emergence of cognition and the self, has been elaborated within the discipline of neurobiology by Antonio Damasio. See *Descartes' Error: Emotion, Reason, and the Human Brain* (New York: Penguin, 1994); *The Feeling of What Happens: Body and Emotions in the Making of Consciousness* (New York: Harcourt, 1999); *Looking for Spinoza: Joy, Sorrow, and the Feeling Brain* (Orlando: Harcourt, 2003); *Self Comes to Mind: Constructing the Conscious Mind* (New York: Pantheon, 2010); *Feeling and Knowing: Making Minds Conscious* (New York: Pantheon, 2021).

For the links of Schmitz's theories to early Western and Asian ideas, see Guido Rappe, *Archaische Leiberfahrung: Der Leib in der frühgriechischen Philosophie und in aussereuropäischen Kulturen* (Berlin: Akademie Verlag, 1995) (*qi* is discussed in Ch. 5); Georg Berkemer and Guido Rappe, ed., *Das Herz im Kulturvergleich* (Akademie Verlag, 1996). On the Homeric depiction of the interaction of body and spirit, see Michael Clarke, *Flesh and Spirit in the Songs of Homer: A Study of Words and Myths* (Oxford: Oxford University Press, 1999).

On the way in which early Chinese theories of the embodied self interact with some current Western ideas, see Raphals, *Tripartite Self*, "Conclusions."

[13] George Lakoff and Mark Johnson, *Philosophy in the Flesh: The Embodied Mind and Its Challenge to Western Thought* (New York: Basic Books, 1999); Johnson, *The Body in the Mind: The Bodily Basis of Meaning, Imagination, and Reason* (Chicago: University of Chicago Press, 1987); *The Meaning of the Body: Aesthetics of Human Understanding* (Chicago: University of Chicago Press, 2007);

Cultivating the Embodied Self through Philosophy

Cultivating an embodied self to attain a correct, healthy person emerged as a topic in China (as it had in Europe) in the philosophical texts of the fourth century BCE.[14,15] One major form of this was the articulation of ritual performances (*li* 禮) as a model for human, bodily action. The clearest expressions of such ideas were speeches attributed to speakers in the *Zuo zhuan*,

---

Daniela Vallega-Neu, *The Bodily Dimension in Thinking* (Albany: SUNY Press, 2005); Kuang-ming Wu, *On Chinese Body Thinking: A Cultural Hermeneutic* (Leiden: Brill, 1997); Richard Zaner, *The Problem of Embodiment*, 2nd ed. (The Hague: Martinus Nijhoff, 1971) (this examines embodied thought in Sartre and Merleau-Ponty); Annie Murphy Paul, *The Extended Mind: The Power of Thinking Outside the Brain* (Boston: Houghton Mifflin Hardcourt, 2021); Joshua Sokol, "The Thoughts of a Spiderweb," *Quanta Magazine*, May 22, 2017.

[14] A similar approach to dividing the study of early Chinese cultivation of the embodied self into three (four if one includes the late Eastern Han) distinct approaches, each pursued by a distinct "community" involved in forms of "Daoism" is elaborated in Michael, *Philosophical Enactment and Bodily Cultivation in Early Daoism*, ch. 3. The three forms are 1) "Yangsheng 養生 Daoism" in which reclusive master-disciple groups cultivated bodily capacities in the mountains, 2) "Fangxian 方仙 Daoism" in which masters of esoteric recipes and healing techniques treat their patients, and 3) "Huang Lao 黃老 Daoism" in which members of Warring States philosophical lineage acted as public intellectuals in shaping elite conduct and imperial policies.

[15] Michael Stanley-Baker, "Health and Philosophy in Pre- and Early Imperial China," in *Health: A History*, ed. Peter Adamson (Oxford: Oxford University Press, 2019), pp. 7–42; John Emerson, "Yang Chu's Discovery of the Body," *Philosophy East and West* 46.4: 533–566 (1996). For a broader treatment of the centrality in early Chinese thought of cultivating body and self, see Paul Fischer, *Self-Cultivation in Early China* (Albany: SUNY Press, 2022).

On the idea that philosophy in ancient Greece and Rome was not simply a set of ideas, but rather a way of life to totally re-create the self as a superior being within a group, see Pierre Hadot, *What Is Ancient Philosophy?* tr. Michael Chase (Cambridge, Mass.: Harvard University Press, 2002); *Philosophy as a Way of Life*, tr. Chase (Oxford, Blackwell, 1995); *La Citadelle intérieure: Introduction aux Pensées de Marc Aurèle* (Paris: Fayard, 1997); Ilsetraut Hadot, *Seneca und die griechisch-römisch Tradition der Seelenleitung* (Berlin: Walter de Gruyter, 1969); Martha Nussbaum, *The Therapy of Desire: Theory and Practice in Hellenistic Ethics* (Princeton: Princeton University Press, 1994); Nussbaum, ed., *The Poetics of Therapy: Hellenistic Ethics in Its Rhetorical and Literary Context*, *Apeiron: A Journal for Ancient Philosophy and Science* XXIII:4 (December, 1990); Philip J. van der Eijk, *Medicine and Philosophy in Classical Antiquity: Doctors and Philosophers on Nature, Soul, Health and Disease* (Cambridge: Cambridge University Press, 2005); James A. Francis, *Subversive Virtue: Asceticism and Authority in the Second-Century Pagan World* (University Park: The Pennsylvania State University Press, 1995).

Inspired by Hadot, Foucault late in his career elaborated a theory of ancient philosophy as, among other things, an attempt to master the body to create a perfected self. See Foucault, *The Use of Pleasure*, tr. Robert Hurley (New York: Pantheon Books, 1985); *The Care of the Self*, tr. Hurley (New York: Vintage Books, 1986); *L'Origine de l'herméneutique de soi: Conférences prononcées à Dartmouth College, 1980* (Paris: Vrin, 2013); *L'Herméneutique du sujet: Cours au Collège de France, 1981–1982* (Paris: Gallimard, 2001); *Le Gouvernement de soi et des autres: Cours au Collège de France, 1982–1983* (Paris: Gallimard, 2008). On these ideas, see Wolfgang Detel, *Foucault and Classical Antiquity: Power, Ethics and Knowledge*, tr. David Wigg-Wolf (Cambridge: Cambridge University Press, 2005).

a historical work from this time. Some speeches in this text argued that the roles that defined the self directed the body's *qi*. Thus, the head of the Jin ruler's kitchen explained that food drove the body's energies, which filled the ruler's fixed resolve (*zhi* 志) and fixed his speech for making commands.[16] This idea that controlling bodily *qi* was crucial to performing social roles also figured in military texts, where energies drove troops to fight and intensified their resolve.[17] Roel Sterckx has extensively analyzed the relationship of cooking and sacrifice to self-cultivation, morality, and sagehood.[18]

The idea that the body's energies drive the fulfilment of social roles is also articulated by Zichan, a leading minister in Zheng state. He argues that rituals provide models for all human actions, guiding the body's *qi* to produce fixed resolve.[19] The idea that rituals are the basis of life and fundamental to human existence recurs throughout the *Zuo zhuan*, which links these to the body and its *qi*.[20] Thus one speaker argues that ritual is essential to becoming a "complete human" (*cheng ren* 成人), others state that it is the trunk of the body/self (*shen*), and others use failings in ritual as a sign predicting imminent death, sometimes linking ritual and death through the embodied nature of the former. Other passages argue that ritual protected the body, or that it was the "carriage" of government which protected the body.[21]

Speakers also argued that only through ritual can the ruler value his own body, which is necessary to his caring for the state, or that the ruler's valuing his body is essential to protecting his people.[22] These ideas resemble those later attributed to followers of Yang Zhu, who argued that only one who placed supreme value on his own body, not allowing it to be harmed in any way, was qualified to rule a state.

---

16 [*Chun qiu*] *Zuo zhuan zhu* 春秋左轉注, ed. Yang Bojun 楊伯峻 (Beijing: Zhonghua, 1983), Zhao 9, p. 1312. On proper cooking producing a proper heart/mind, see also Zhao 20, pp. 1419–1420; Zhao 25, pp. 1457–1458.

17 On military texts, see Lewis, *Sanctioned Violence*, ch. 6. On *qi* guiding the *zhi* in the *Zuo zhuan*, see Xi 22, p. 398. For related passages in the *Zuo zhuan*, see Lewis, *The Construction of Space* (Albany: SUNY Press, 2006), p. 29, 322, note 70. On ritual and the body, see also pp. 30–32.

18 Sterckx, "Le Pouvoir des Sens: Sagesse et Perception Sensorielle en Chine Ancienne," in *Cahiers d'Institut Marcel Granet* 1 (Paris: Presses Universitaires de France, 2003), pp. 71–92; Sterckx, ed., *Of Tripod and Palate: Food, Politics, and Religion in Traditional China* (New York: Palgrave-MacMillan, 2005); "Sages, Cooks and Flavours in Warring States and Han China," *Monumenta Serica* 54 (2006): 1–46; *Food, Sacrifice, and Sagehood in Early China* (Cambridge: Cambridge University Press, 2011).

19 *Zuo zhuan zhu*, Zhao 25, pp. 1458–1459. Zichan identifies "six *qi*" linked with the emotions, and discusses how rituals guide all the basic emotions.

20 Lewis, *Writing and Authority in Early China* (Albany: SUNY Press, 1999), pp. 133–140.

21 *Zuo zhuan zhu*, Wen 15, pp. 612, 614; Cheng 13, pp. 860 (2), 860–861; Cheng 15, p. 873 (2); Zhao 1, pp. 1219, 1220–1221; Zhao 7, p. 1295. This link between ritual and body is sometimes demonstrated through graphically linking *li* 禮 and *ti* 體, perhaps entailing a phonetic relation, or interchanging them. See Lewis, *The Construction of Space*, p. 323 note 79.

22 *Zuo zhuan zhu*, Cheng 15, p. 873; Zhao 25, p. 1455.

This idea, cited in the *Mencius* and elaborated in the Western Han *Huainanzi*, was given its fullest expression in the third-century BCE text, *Springs and Autumns of Master Lü.*[23] The idea that ritual underpinned human society through educating the embodied self was also developed in the third-century BCE *Xunzi.*[24]

Another text that discussed the embodied self in the fourth century BCE was the *Mencius*. Probably most influential was its account of the "four sprouts" in the heart/mind that underlay the development of the primary moral virtues. These four sprouts, which were fundamental to the *Mencius*'s argument that human nature was good, were placed in parallel to the four limbs, thus treating the heart/mind as part of the physical body. Other passages treat the heart/mind in the same way, paralleling mental problems to a crooked finger, or claiming that the mind's virtues radiated from the countenance and invigorated the limbs.[25] This embodied heart/mind also figured in a division of the body into higher and lower parts, with the heart/mind ruling over the limbs and the stomach. This in turn justified the social hierarchy in which those who worked with their minds ruled those who worked with their physical strength.[26]

One final meditation on the body is Mencius's discourse on his "flood-like [*hao ran* 浩然] *qi*." After discussing attaining a heart/mind that did not become agitated, Mencius argued that his flood-like *qi* if properly nourished could fill the cosmos, but that it must be fed with moral virtues. The "fixed intent" is the commander of the *qi*, which fills the body, while moral errors lead to an unease that starves the body's energies.[27] This argument thus uses the same categories as the *Zuo zhuan*, but it reverses the order of priority in making intent superior to *qi*.

In the same century, the poem "Inner Training" (*nei ye* 內業), which is included in the *Guanzi*, developed a model of purifying the embodied self as a center from which cultivated energies could be projected through the cosmos.[28] This expounds transforming the entire person, beginning with correctly placing the

[23] Lewis, *The Construction of Space*, pp. 14–19.

[24] Paul Rakita Goldin, *Rituals of the Way: The Philosophy of Xunzi* (Chicago: Open Court, 1999), esp. ch. 1.

[25] *Mengzi zheng yi* 孟子正義, ed. Jiao Xun 焦循, in *Xin bian zhuzi ji cheng*, vol. 1 (Taipei: Shijie Shuju, 1974) IIA, "Gongsun Chou shang," pp. 238–239; VIA, "Gaozi shang," pp. 450–451, 464; VIIA, "Jin xin shang," pp. 534–535.

[26] *Mengzi zheng yi*, IIIA, "Teng Wen Gong shang," p. 219; VIA, "Gaozi shang," pp. 466–467, 467. Other passages state that the Shang and Zhou founders "embodied" (*shen* 身) the virtues, only sages fully employ their bodies' capacities, and one who fully realizes his heart/mind cultivates his embodied self (*shen*) until death. See VIIA "Jin xin shang," pp. 517, 544, 552. Raphals, *Tripartite Self*, devotes considerable attention to the tendency of philosophical texts to insist that the heart/mind should ideally act as ruler, in contrast to texts on "nourishing life" or medicine.

[27] *Mengzi zheng yi*, IIA, "Gongsun Chou shang," pp. 214–219. The link between the environment and the body through *qi* is also discussed in VIIA, "Jin xin shang," p. 550. For other passages on how personal energies might fill the cosmos, see Lewis, *Construction of Space*," p. 320 note 53.

[28] Harold Roth, *Original Tao*: *Inward Training (Nei-yeh) and the Foundations of Taoist Mysticism* (New York: Columbia University Press, 1999); A. C. Graham, *Disputers of the Tao*:

body, working through the sense organs to the mind, and culminating in the gathering of refined energies that transformed the body and radiated outward. The primary dangers were the sense organs, emotions, desires, and worries which disturbed the heart/mind's tranquility. The text refers to political attainments such as ruling the myriad things, imposing tasks upon others, ordering the world, and making it submit not through punishments and rewards but through the flow of bodily energies from a stabilized mind. However, such considerations remain marginal to the text, which emphasizes self-perfection.[29]

This poem was influential, as demonstrated by citations and elaborations in other texts, including the *Mencius*. Most importantly, it was adapted into political discussions in the chapters "Techniques of the Heart/Mind" (*xin shu shang* and *xia*, 新書上下) that were also included in the *Guanzi*. The latter of these chapters, sometimes described as a commentary on the "Inner Training," follows quotations from the poem with accounts of how the sage rules all things, how the peace of his heart/mind produces order and peace in the state, how the people are restrained not through his anger and punishments but because he follows the Way from its origins, how his transformed body carries Heaven and embodies the Earth, and how his completed heart/mind illumines and comprehends the entire world.[30]

"Techniques of the Heart/Mind I" is not so thoroughly mapped onto the "Inner Training," but it adopts passages from it, and it begins with the argument that if the ruler strays from the Way, due to being possessed by emotions or sense impressions, then his subordinates will fail. It also argues that the ruler will hold to his position if he attains self-control through quiescence, and that the Great Way will achieve peace although it cannot be spoken. Like the Mawangdui corpus associated with the Yellow Emperor (see below), it states that laws emerged from this Way.[31] The "Inner Training" resembled the *Laozi*, except that the latter became more focused on political matters among many

---

Philosophical Argument in Ancient China (La Salle: Open Court, 1989), pp. 100–105; Lewis, *Construction of Space*, pp. 20–29.

29 *Guanzi jiao zhu* 管子校注, ed. Li Xiangfeng 梨翔鳳, in *Xin bian zhuzi ji cheng* (Beijing: Wenwu, 2004), ch. 16.49, pp. 937, 939, 943. In arguing that the ruler commands through the power of his perfected self, rather than with rewards and punishment, the "Inner Training" differs from the later *Han Feizi* which argued that self-transformation culminated in the ability to punish and reward according to objective standards free from personal sentiments.

30 *Guanzi jiao zhu*, ch. 13.37, pp. 778–779, 780, 781–782, 783. Links between the body of the ruler and his state are also discussed in Cook, *Medicine and Healing in Early China*, pp. 21–28, 40–42; Robin D. S. Yates, "Body, Space, Time and Bureaucracy: Boundary Creation and Control Mechanisms in Early China," in *Boundaries in China: Critical Views*, ed. J. Hay (London: Reaktion Books, 1994), pp. 56–80.

31 *Guanzi jiao zhu*, ch. 13.36, pp. 759–760 (3), 764, 767 (2), 770 (2), 771, 776 (2). See also Romain Graziani, "De la régence du monde à la souveraineté intérieure: Une Étude des quatre chapitres de 'L'art de l'esprit' du *Guanzi*," Ph.D. dissertation, Université Paris VII, 2001.

adherents, and this political shift of contemplative self-perfecting was highlighted in the *Han Feizi*, as will be discussed in the following paragraphs.[32]

The idea that self-cultivation was essential to the ruler was not limited to texts linked to the "Inner Training." The *Xunzi*, while offering "ritual" as an alternative to bio-spiritual practices as a "technique of the body," argued in its later chapters that disturbances aroused by emotions and desires had to be mastered so that the ruler could perform his roles. Notably, the method of attaining such mastery is also referred to as the "techniques of the heart/mind." The discussion of mental self-mastery in the chapter "Eliminating Blockage" states:

> What creates blockage? Desires [*yu* 欲] create blockage, aversion [*wù* 惡] creates blockage, beginnings create blockage, endings create blockage, distance creates blockage, closeness creates blockage, breadth creates blockage, shallowness creates blockage, antiquity creates blockage, and modernity creates blockage. Wherever objects differ, they mutually create blockage. This is the universal calamity for the "techniques of the heart/mind."[33]

This is followed by a list of past rulers who failed because some obsession blocked their ability to perceive and respond to the actual situation. In this chapter, the "techniques of the heart/mind" refers to a mental control that eliminates desires and dislikes, removing the distinctions that create fixation. Only the sage escapes such blockages:

> The sage recognizes the calamities that befall the "techniques of the heart/mind" and perceives the disaster of being blocked. Therefore, he has no desires or loathing, treats nothing as a beginning or an end, nothing as near or far, nothing as broad or shallow, nothing as ancient or modern. He lays out everything and precisely sets it in the balance.[34]

Through controlling his mental responses and transcending all the distinctions by which people carve up the world before falling into preferences for one side, the sage makes correct judgments.

Elsewhere the *Xunzi* offers another version of a technique of the heart/mind. It begins with a rubric: "the technique of regulating the vital energies and nourishing the heart/mind" (*zhi qi yang xin zhi shu* 治氣養心之術), which echoes the chapters in the *Guanzi*. After listing therapies for defects of temperament and

[32] Roth, *Original Tao*, 186–190. Pages 190–203 are also relevant.

[33] *Xunzi ji jie* 荀子集解, ed. Wang Xianqian 王先謙 (1842–1918), in *Xin bian zhuzi ji cheng*, vol. 2 (Taipei: Shijie, 1974), ch. 15.21, p. 259. A passage on page 258 echoes or anticipates passages in "Techniques of the Heart/Mind I." Ori Tavor argues that the *Xunzi* argued against rival models of mental and bodily cultivation in "Xunzi's Theory of Ritual Revisited: Reading Ritual as Corporal Technology," printed online (Dordrecht: Springer Science, 2013).

[34] *Xunzi ji jie*, ch. 15.21, p. 263.

thought – most associated with intemperate or violent responses, or guile in calculations – it concludes:

> For all techniques employed to regulate one's vital energies and nourish the heart/mind, nothing is more direct or rapid than ritual, nothing is more important than obtaining a teacher, and nothing is more miraculously transformative [*shen* 神] than unifying your loves.[35]

Here the technique of "nourishing" the heart/mind culminates in mastering one's likes (and presumably dislikes), but it takes a "Confucian" turn by basing these on the guidance of ritual and a teacher. Another passage links nourishing the heart/mind with total concentration and sincerity (*cheng* 誠). This perfected inner state, the central virtue in the "Zhongyong" [中庸] chapter of the *Li ji*, achieves self-mastery where the true gentleman matches Heaven: silent but understood, never giving but regarded as generous, and never angry but held in awe. This mental state also allows him to "carefully preserve his solitude/concentration" (*shen qi du* 慎其獨), a capacity discussed in the "Wu xing pian" (五行篇) found at Mawangdui and Guodian. In these texts, it indicates an ability to escape the dominance of sense impressions and concern for externals, creating a virtuous power that makes one a match for Heaven.[36]

This text (whose earlier version comes from a tomb that probably dates to the early third century BCE) again elaborates the *embodied* self as central to moral discourse and sagehood. As discussed by Mark Csikszentmihalyi, the "Wu xing pian" responded to critiques of the hypocritical and self-serving nature of the *ru* program of ritual and learning by elaborating a theory of the motivations for good action, and of its physical manifestations in the fleshly body. This theory distinguishes actions which "take form internally," and hence are "virtuous" (*de* 德), from those which do not and are merely objectively "good" (*shan* 善). It elaborates the sequence of mental states – beginning with "worry" (*you* 憂) and "longing" (*si* 思), and ending with "delight [in virtue]" (*le* 樂) – which make possible the modes of thinking – "focusing on essentials" (*jing* 景), "attention to long-term consequences" (*chang* 長), and "directness" (*jing* 徑) – that culminate in the virtues.

The text also stresses that this process entails training the senses in visual and aural moral differentiations, so that one becomes "clear-sighted" (*ming* 明) in perceiving the Way, and "sharp-eared" (*cong* 聰) in hearing it, and thus wise enough to recognize its worth. Finally, this internally generated virtuous wisdom manifests itself in a "jade coloration" (*yu se* 玉色) and a "jade tone" (*yin* 音)

---

35 *Xunzi ji jie*, ch. 1.2, p. 15.

36 *Xunzi ji jie*: 2.3, pp. 28–29. On the passages in both versions of the "Wu xing pian," see Mark Csikszentmilhaly I, *Material Virtue*: *Ethics and the Body in Early China* (Leiden: E. J. Brill, 2004), pp. 287–288, 321–323. The idea is discussed on pp. 78–81, 174.

which make one's perfected virtues both visible and audible to others sufficiently self-cultivated to recognize it. This ultimate level – where the virtues, the senses, and the body all achieve perfection – is sagehood.[37]

The text is related to the *Mencius* (as well as the "Zhongyong"), sharing the idea that the virtues are aspects of an integrated person in whom the sprouting virtues grow along with the physical limbs, and the cultivated moral character shines through the flesh. This cultivation of an embodied self also relies on practicing rituals, thus developing ideas from the *Zuo zhuan*. As Csikszentmilhayi argues, this "material virtue" tradition that linked physiological changes to the impact of moral motivations was also "facilitated by interactions with burgeoning technical disciplines of medicine and physiognomy," an interplay whose further developments will be discussed later in this essay.[38]

At the end of the Warring States, the *Han Feizi* incorporated this idea of a distinctive regime for self-transformation into a program for creating the ideal ruler. The beginning of "The Way of the Ruler" (*zhu dao* 主道), a lengthy rhyming passage patterned on the *Dao de jing*, follows a passage describing the cosmic Way, to which the ruler must assimilate himself:

> "Eliminate loves and hates [*hào wù*],
> The officials then show their true, simple nature [素 *sù*]."
> Eliminate cunning; eliminate deliberate action
> The people will then restrain themselves.
> Having intelligence, he does not use it to think,
> Causing all things to each know their own place.
> Having a worthy character, he does not use it to act,
> So he can observe the motivations of his officials.
> Having courage, he does not become angry,
> Causing his officials to fully use their martial abilities.
> By eliminating his intelligence, he is enlightened.
> By eliminating his worthiness, he achieves merit.
> By eliminating his courage, he becomes strong.[39]

[37] Csikszentmilhayi, *Material Virtue*, ch. 3. On the relation of mind and body in this text, see also Fan Limei 范麗梅, *Yan zhe shen zhi wen: Guodian xieben guanjian zi yu shen xin sixiang* 言者身之文:郭店寫本關鍵字與身心思想 (Taipei: Taibei Daxue Chubanshe Zhongxin, 2017), ch. 1, 3, 4. On the heart/mind and body in the Guodian texts, see Kuan-yun Huang, *The Lost Texts of Confucius' Grandson*: *Guodian, Zisi, and Beyond* (Hong Kong: The Chinese University of Hong Kong Press, 2023). On the senses and wisdom in early China, see Jane Geaney, *On the Epistemology of the Senses in Early Chinese Thought* (Honolulu: University of Hawai'i Press, 2002); Irmgard Enzinger, *Ausdruck und Eindruck: Zum chineschischen Verständnis der Sinne* (Wiesbaden: Harrassowitz Verlag, 2006). See also Geaney, *Language as Bodily Practice in Early China*: *A Chinese Grammatology* (Albany: SUNY Press, 2018).

[38] On the *Mencius* and the "Wu xing pian," see Csikszentmilhayi, *Material Virtue*, ch. 3. On the ideal of the sage's perfected body, see ch. 4.

[39] *Han Feizi xin jiao zhu* 韓非子新校注, ed. Chen Qiyou (Shanghai: Shanghai Guji Chubanshe, 2000), ch. 1.5, p. 66. The chapter continues to elaborate these ideas through p. 81. The

This echoes stanza 19 of the received *Laozi*, and follows it in arguing that the ruler must through self-cultivation eliminate personal ideas, sentiments, and desires. Still and empty, he allows things, above all his officials, to fulfil their roles.[40] Applied to things, this allows each object to assume its proper place; applied to people, it lets them reveal their true capacities and desires, forcing them to serve the ruler or face elimination.

Remaining hidden and mysterious, the ruler causes his subordinates to devote themselves to proposing and carrying out ideas. As they compete in presenting ideas, he sees with all the eyes in the empire, hears with its ears, and thinks with the minds of the sages without himself being a sage. Thus, the text incorporates the same model as the "Wu xing pian," where perfecting eyes and ears, here through political mastery, enables the emergence of a sage.[41] The theme of the ruler's being hidden, which became fundamental to the spatial order of Chinese politics, figures throughout this discussion.[42]

Subsequent chapters reiterate many themes from the "Way of the Ruler," while adding new emphases. "Brandishing Authority," which again is largely in verse like the *Laozi*, precedes its discussion of the ruler remaining hidden and still by describing the sensual and emotional attractions from which he must first free himself.[43] This conquering of sensual desires to keep the body's energies intact is the first step to establishing the empty and undisturbed interior of the ruler at the center of all things. This echoes not only the *Laozi* (as emphasized later in the *Han Feizi*'s commentary), but also the texts related to "Inner Training" which emphasized establishing a still center from which the ruler's influence radiated through the world.

proposition that if the ruler eliminates his own hates and loves, then the officials revert to simplicity also appears in "The Two Handles." See *Han Feizi xin jiao zhu*, ch. 2.7, p. 132.

40 *Laozi dao de jing* 老子道德經, ed. Wang Bi 王弼 (CE 226–249), commentary by Lu Deming 陸德明 (CE 556–627), in *Xin bian zhuzi ji cheng*, vol. 3, p. 10. Subsequent sections of this chapter of the *Han Feizi* echo stanza 52, p. 32; stanzas 20, 21, 25, pp. 11–12, 14; stanza 67, p. 41; stanza 73, p. 43; stanza 27, p. 15. Three of these seven stanzas appear in the Guodian material related to the *Laozi*. See Guo Yi 郭沂, *Guodian zhujian yu xian-Qin xueshu sixiang* 郭店竹簡與先秦學術思想 (Shanghai: Shanghai Jiaoyu Chubanshe, 2001), pp. 50, 106, 112.

41 In contrast, the ruler's using his own vision, hearing, and cogitation to supervise his ministers would allow them to manipulate him. See *Han Feizi xin jiao zhu*, ch. 2.6, p. 107.

42 On hiding the ruler to generate power, see Lewis, *Construction of Space*, pp. 114–118. On the ruler remaining hidden, and keeping his ideas and emotions secret, see also *Han Feizi xin jiao zhu*, ch. 1.5, p. 74, in a passage that begins "The Way lies in being invisible."

43 *Han Feizi xin jiao zhu*, ch. 2.8, p.137. This link of the mastery of sensual experience with the establishment of the ruler at the center also appears in "Illustrating Laozi." See ch. 7.21, p. 449: "The orifices of the senses are the door and windows of essential spirit [*jing shen*]. When ears and eyes are exhausted through sounds and colors, the quintessential energies will be exhausted by external attractions, and the center will have no ruler."

The idea that mental tranquility leads to physical completeness and culminates in political power is given its clearest expression in the chapter "Explaining Laozi [*jie lao* 解老]":

> "Virtuous power [*de* 德]" is on the inside. "Obtaining [*de* 得]" is on the outside. [When the *Laozi* says] "the highest virtue is not treated as virtue," this means that his spirit [*shen*] does not overflow [*yin* 淫] outward. If the spirit does not overflow outward, then the body is complete. The body being complete is called "virtuous power." "Virtuous power" means to "obtain" the [entire] body. Virtuous power is always collected through being without conscious action [*wu wei*] and made complete through having no desires. It attains peace through not pondering and becomes firm through not being used. If you act or desire, then the virtuous power has no place to lodge [舍 *she*, the term referring to the cleansed mind in the "Inner Training"].[44]

By purging all mental activity, both emotional and intellectual, the ruler preserves his body's energetic resources, which in turn form the power that allows him to command the world from his own center. The theme of the ruler stilling all mental activity to keep body and spirit intact, and thereby command all, recurs throughout this chapter. This perfection of the ruler's embodied self also results in his superior health and extended longevity. The common people, in contrast, are dominated by desires and feelings, which wastes their energies and destroys their bodies.[45]

This chapter concludes with a lengthy passage on appropriate responses to objects, emotional mastery, a perfected body, and political power:

> The sage is different. Having once settled his inclinations or aversions, when he sees some object that he loves, it cannot drag him. Since he cannot be dragged astray, this is called [in the *Laozi*] "not pulled out." Being entirely unified in his emotions, even when he sees something desirable, his spirit is not disturbed. . . .

---

44 *Han Feizi xin jiao zhu*, ch. 6.20, p. 370. On the *Han Feizi*'s explications of the *Laozi*, see Sarah Queen, "Han Feizi and the Old Master: A Comparative Analysis and Translation of Han Feizi Chapter 20, 'Jie Lao', and Chapter 21, 'yu Lao'," in *Dao Companion to the Philosophy of Han Fei*, ed. Paul R. Goldin (Cham: Springer, 2013), pp. 197–256; Michael, *Philosophical Enactment and Bodily Cultivation in Early Daoism*, pp. 124–126, 140, 246.

45 *Han Feizi xin jiao zhu*, ch. 6.20, pp. 374, 376, 380, 387, 388, 390 (the sage ruler obtains a "complete body" and consequently "long life"), pp. 394 (acuity of senses as celestial), 395 (the emotional agitation of ordinary people wastes their spirit, in contrast with the sage's tranquility), p. 396 (keeping the senses clear through mastering desires accumulates harmonious *qi*), p. 397 (links preserving the state with preserving the body), pp. 398–399, 402–403 (a well-regulated state results in the people's blood and *qi* being well-regulated), 405, 407–408 (only the sage ruler avoids the desire for sensual pleasures that produce disorder and calamity, while the people's worries produce diseases), pp. 416–417 (the sage ruler alone does not waste his spirit energies and so remains safe and healthy), p. 421 (people expend themselves on what they love, while the ruler keeps his energies replete), p. 423.

> His body thereby accumulates refined energies that become virtuous power. The household thereby turns wealth into resources that become virtuous power. The village, state, and world all use their people to become virtuous power.
>
> Now if you regulate the body/self, then external objects cannot throw your refined, spirit energies into disorder. So [the *Laozi*] says, "Cultivating the body/self, the virtuous power is then perfected." If you thus regulate the household, then useless objects cannot disturb calculations, and resources will be abundant.... If those who regulate a state practice this discipline, this will increase the number of villages that have virtuous power, so [the *Laozi*] says, "Cultivating it in the state, its virtuous power will be plentiful." If the ruler of a world empire practices this discipline, then all living things will flourish from his influence, so [the *Laozi*] says, "Cultivating in the world [*tianxia* 天下] its virtuous power will be universal."[46]

The sage's ability to escape emotional responses to objects leads to bodily perfection, a regulated household, flourishing villages, and finally a perfected world. This extension of virtuous power follows in reverse the same series as the opening of the "Da xue" [大學).[47] Moreover, the self in both these texts creates

[46] *Han Feizi xin jiao zhu*, ch. 6.20, pp. 428–429.

[47] *Li ji zhu shu* 禮記注疏, in *Shisan jing zhushu* 十三經注疏, vol. 5 (Taipei: Yiwen, 1974), ch. 60:42, pp. 1a–2b. This process, like the *Han Feizi* and the "Wu Xing pian," also aims at achieving the radiating of virtuous power, and like the "Wu xing pian" it also insists (twice) that the true gentleman must "carefully preserve his solitude/concentration" (*shen qi du*) to attain the necessary state of total concentration and sincerity (*cheng*).

The ruler's body – theological, ritual, political, or charismatic – and its relation to the "body politic" has been the subject of much scholarship. Best known is Ernest H. Kantorowicz, *The King's Two Bodies*: *A Study in Mediaeval Political Theology* (Princeton: Princeton University Press, 1957). This has inspired Alain Boureau, *Histoires d'un historien: Kantorowicz* (Paris: Gallimard, 1990); *Le simple corps du roi: L'impossible sacralité des souverains français* (Paris: Les Éditions de Paris, 2000); David Starkey, "Representation through Intimacy: A Study in the Symbolism of Monarchy and Court Office in Early-Modern England," in *Symbols and Sentiments: Cross-Cultural Studies in Symbolism*, ed. I. Lewis (London: Academic Press, 1977), pp. 187–224; Starkey, ed., *The English Court*: *From the War of the Roses to the Civil War* (London: Longman, 1987); Lawrence Normand, "The Miraculous Body in James VI and I, Jonson and Shakespeare," in *The Body in Late Medieval and Early Modern Culture*, ed. Darryll Grantley and Nina Taunton (Aldershot: Ashgate, 2000), pp. 143–156; Sergio Bertelli, *The King's Body: Sacred Rituals of Power in Medieval and Early Modern Europe*, tr. R. Burr Litchfield (University Park: Pennsylvania State University Press, 2001); Sarah E. Melzer and Kathryn Norberg, eds., *From the Royal to the Republican Body*: *Incorporating the Political in Seventeenth- and Eighteenth-Century France* (Berkeley: University of California Press, 1998); David McNally, *Blood and Money*: *War, Slavery, Finance, and Empire* (Chicago: Haymarket Books, 2020), ch. 2–3. On the Roman empire and medieval Christianity, see Mary Beard and John Henderson, "The Emperor's New Body: Ascension from Rome," in *Parchments of Gender: Deciphering the Body in Antiquity* (Oxford: Clarendon Press, 1998), pp. 191–220; Mark W. Hamilton, *The Body Royal*: *The Social Poetics of Kingship in Ancient Israel* (Leiden: Brill, 2005); Sarah Beckwith, *Christ's Body*: *Identity, Culture and Society in Late Medieval Writings* (London: Routledge, 1993), ch. 2; Agostino Parvinci-Bagliani, *The Pope's Body*, tr. David S. Peterson (Chicago: University of Chicago Press, 2000); Boureau, *La papesse Jeanne* (Paris: Aubier, 1988); Jean-Louis Chrétien, *Symbolique du corps*: *La tradition chrétienne du* Cantique des Cantiques (Paris: Presses Universitaires de France, 2005). See also three articles in *Fragments for a History of the Human Body*, vol. 3, pp. 387–447. These are Luc de Heusch, "The Sacrificial Body of

its power and expands its reach through the relationships that define the person within the field-focus model.

The opposition between emotion, which binds people to particular commitments, and the objective standards of the common good is also read into the cosmic patterns for proper government in "Great Principles [大體 *da ti*]." First invoking Heaven, Earth, the four seasons, and natural phenomena as models, it enumerates the necessity of law, techniques of administration, rewards and punishments, and objective standards, and concludes:

> Therefore the "Great Man" lodges his body between Heaven and Earth, and the world's objects are complete. He passes his heart/mind through the mountains and seas, and the state is rich. The ruler has no poison of anger, and the subjects no calamity of submerged resentment, so ruler and ruled join in unspoiled simplicity, taking the Way as their lodging.[48]

Here the ruler is modeled on the "Great Man" described in the *Zhuangzi*, suppressing his personal sentiments and concerns in imitating Heaven and implementing a pure, objective law applied to all things. This provides another version of the fusion of the Way and law-based administration in the perfected person of the ideal ruler.

In addition to accounts of the "Great Man," the *Zhuangzi* offered several other versions of perfected selves. First, later chapters invoked a theory of self-transformation by a ruler wielding "techniques of the heart/mind" like those in the *Guanzi* and *Xunzi*:

> The root is in the ruler, and the branch tip in the subordinates; the essential is in the ruler, and the details in the subordinates. The use of armies and weapons is the branch tip of innate power [*de*]. Rewards and punishments, benefitting and harming, the five mutilating punishments are the branch tips of teaching. Rituals, laws, measures, numbers, administrative terminology, and matching of details, these are the branch tips of governance. The sounds of bells and drums, the look of feathers and banners, these are the branch tips of music. Weeping and graded degrees of mourning costume, these are the branch tips of grieving. As for these five branch tips, only when [the ruler] uses his refined spirit energies [*jing shen*] and sets into motion his "techniques of the heart/mind," can they be pursued.[49]

---

the King"; Florence Dupont, "The Emperor-God's Other Body"; and Louis Marin, "The Body-of-Power and Incarnation at Port Royal and in Pascal or of the Figurability of the Political Absolute."

48 *Han Feizi xin jiao zhu*, ch. 8.29, pp. 555, 559. On the "Great Man," see Graham, *Disputers of the Tao*, pp. 204–211. On this figure's later evolution, see Donald Holzman, *Poetry and Politics: The Life and Works of Juan Chi* (Cambridge: Cambridge University Press, 1976), ch. 10.

49 *Zhuangzi ji shi* 莊子集釋, commentaries by Guo Xiang 郭象 (CE 252–312) and Lu Deming 陸德明 (CE 556–627), ed. Guo, Qingfan 郭慶藩, in *Xin bian zhuzi ji cheng*, vol. 3 (Taipei: Shijie, 1974), ch. 13, p. 209. On concepts of the body in the *Zhuangzi*, see Deborah Sommer, "Concepts of the Body in the *Zhuangzi*," in *Experimental Essays on Zhuangzi*, ed. Victor Mair, 2nd ed. (Dunedin: Three Pines Press, 2010), pp. 212–228.

This portrays contemporary political and social practices as inadequate, offering instead an idealized ruler whose mastery of the "techniques of the heart/mind" allows his accumulation of mental energies.

Chapter 12 of the *Zhuangzi* likewise describes the true ruler as one who identifies himself with the Way, accumulating inner power that allows him to command the world.[50] Similarly, chapter 13 describes the mind of the sage ruler as being still so that like water or a mirror it reflects all things, and then discusses the ruler who matches perfectly with Heaven and Earth:

> With his united mind in repose, he is king of the world. The spirits do not afflict him and his soul knows no weariness. With his united mind in repose, all things submit – which means that his emptiness and stillness reach throughout the cosmos and penetrate all things. This is called Heavenly joy, through which the sage's mind shepherds the entire world.[51]

This, and the next two chapters of the *Zhuangzi*, sketch other visions of ruling through mastery of the cosmic Way, including citing the vitalizing energy of the ruler's "techniques of the heart/mind" that brings life to the rules and regulations that define government.[52]

A later passage also elaborates a model of the man who becomes ruler of the world through mental self-mastery:

> The one who fixes [within] the Great Serenity emits a Heavenly light. Though he emits a Heavenly light, people see him as a human. When he has cultivated this, he achieves constancy. Because he is constant, people will lodge [*she* 舍, the word applied to the "spirits" in the "Inner Training"] with him, and Heaven will help him. Those people who are lodged are called "Heaven's People," and the man Heaven helps is called the "Son of Heaven."[53]

Here the traditional epithet of the Zhou king indicates a unique relation to Heaven achieved through perfecting internal serenity.

In addition to these discussions of the ruler as a self-perfected being, the *Zhuangzi* also describes humble people who through total concentration and immersion in their surroundings attain mastery of one skill. These figures, whom A. C. Graham names "craftsmen," exemplify an ideal of personhood defined by spontaneously responding to events with an unmatched skill that would be undermined by recourse to thought. These people include carpenters, swimmers, boatmen, cicada-catchers, and most famously Cook Ding who carves innumerable oxen without dulling his

---

50 *Zhuangzi ji shi*, ch. 12, pp. 181–182. See also pp. 192–193.

51 *Zhuangzi ji shi*, ch. 13, pp. 204–205, 207–208.

52 *Zhuangzi ji shi*, ch. 13, pp. 208, 209, 210, 216; ch. 14, pp. 219–220, 222–225.

53 *Zhuangzi ji shi*, ch. 23, p. 344. P. 351 describes how the elimination of emotions and errors induced by sensory experience make the ruler enlightened and empty, and thus able to control all things without deliberate action.

blade because he perceives with his spirit (*shen*) rather than his eyes, and Wheelwright Bian who has a magically efficacious art of crafting a wheel.[54]

A final form of self-perfected persons in the *Zhuangzi* are those who can concentrate their spirit into a trance-like state that leaves mind and body completely void and empty (with a mind being like "ash" and a body like "wood"). One example is the aforementioned cicada-catcher, while others attain this state through "sitting and forgetting" (*zuo wang* 坐忘).[55] Finally, some people are explicitly called "perfected people" (*zhi ren* 至人, sometimes the "perfected people of antiquity"). They are sometimes placed in a hierarchy with the "true people" (*zhen ren* 真人), the "spirit people" (*shen ren* 神人), and the "sages" (*sheng ren* 聖人), usually in that order, indicating declining levels of attainment in self-cultivation. A recurring formula describing the perfected people indicates that their mastery of themselves and the world is such that fires will not burn them, freezing weather chill them, nor anything frighten them.[56] Some can ride clouds and mists to soar freely above the world, which along with the references to spirit trances suggests that ideas in this text were derived from the model of meditation sketched in "Inner Training" and linked to the cult of *xian* immortals that emerged in this period.[57]

In addition to these discussions of the perfected self in the *Zhuangzi* itself, the grave-robbed text purchased by the Shanghai museum "All Things Flow into Form [*fan wu liu xing* 凡物流形], which traces how the ideal ruler cultivates an inner purity that leads to enlightenment, self-possession, and world mastery. As

---

54 Graham, *Disputers of the Tao*, pp. 186–191. See also Mercedes Valmisa, *Adapting: A Chinese Philosophy of Action* (Oxford: Oxford University Press, 2021), pp. 14–30, 59–60, 139–148. On Cook Ding and Wheelwright Bian, see *Zhuangzi ji shi*, ch. 3, pp. 55–58 (the ruler who listens to him expound his art exclaims that he has thereby learned how to "nourish life" [*yang sheng*]; ch. 13, pp. 217–218.

55 *Zhuangzi ji shi*, ch. 2, pp. 21–24; ch. 3, pp. 58–59; ch. 6, pp. 128–129; ch. 19, pp. 281–282 (the cicada-catcher); ch. 21, p. 310 (Laozi in a trance); ch. 23, p. 343. Thomas Michael uses the phrase "*zuo wang*" as his rubric for the *Zhuangzi*'s style of philosophy. See *Philosophical Enactment and Bodily Cultivation in Early Daoism*, pp. 44, 48, 49, 120–122, 139–140.

56 *Zhuangzi ji shi*, ch. 1, p. 11 (the perfected people have no selves, the spirit people no merits, and the sages no fame); ch. 2, pp. 45–46 (on transcending heat, cold, fear, and earthly limits); ch. 4, p. 62; ch. 5, pp. 92–93, 98; ch. 6, p. 102; ch. 7, p. 138 (heart-mind like a mirror that spontaneously responds to everything it encounters, which in ch. 13, p. 204 is attributed to the sage); ch. 13, pp. 216–217; ch. 14, p. 229; ch. 19, pp. 279–280 (imperviousness to fire, water, and fear results from guarding their pure *qi*), 291 (free soaring due to forgetting individual organs), 291–292; ch. 21, pp. 299, 311–312 (becoming a perfect man by achieving a state like animals, moving freely in the world without emotional responses), 312, 316–317 (even in the most perilous situations, his spirit and *qi* are not disturbed); ch. 22, p. 321; ch. 23, pp. 335, 343; ch. 26, p. 404; ch. 29, p. 437; ch. 31, p. 448; ch. 32, p. 454; ch. 33, p. 461 (hierarchy of sage, king, Heavenly man, spirit man, and perfected man).

57 On meditation and the *xian*, with reference to the *Zhuangzi*, see Harper, *Early Chinese Medical Literature*, pp. 112–125, 131.

Kuan-yun Huang has shown, this text has passages that echo or develop many discussions in the received literature, most notably the *Zhuangzi*.[58]

These visions of the perfected self in late Warring States texts such as the *Han Feizi* and the *Zhuangzi* carried forward into the *Huainanzi* in the early Western Han. This syncretic text combined diverse intellectual traditions, but it drew its structuring ideas from, and most frequently cited, the *Laozi* and the *Zhuangzi*. It used these earlier texts to elaborate ideas about the ideal ruler, the perfection of the human body through the purity of its *qi*, and the nature of sages and perfected people. These themes are most explicitly combined in its chapter 7, the "Quintessential Spirit" (*jing shen* 精神).[59] This chapter recapitulates the cosmogonical account of the *Laozi* (already elaborated in ch. 1 of the *Huainanzi*) and then argues that human beings are exalted above other creatures because their *qi* contains the quintessential spirit, the loftiest form of *qi*. Following an account of the human embryo taking shape and being born, it describes the "orbs" (*zang* 藏) within which the bodily *qi* circulates and explains how the human body is a microcosm of Heaven and Earth.[60]

This account of the body's origins leads to a discussion of how superior people, through holding to stillness and eliminating all passions and desires for external objects, can conserve spirit illumination (*shen ming*), perfect their senses, and become a purified spirit. The rest of the chapter develops these ideas, contrasting sages or Perfected People with common people who remain trapped by customs and desires, and waste their bodily energies pursuing wealth and honor. It cites images from the *Zhuangzi*, including how the perfected attain a body "like withered wood" and a "mind like dead ashes"; how they are not harmed by fire, water, or fear; how they do not dream; and how they attain potency (*de*) that gives them world mastery through "techniques of the heart/mind." Near its end the chapter denounces the Confucians and other superficial scholars of its time who devote themselves to studying the Zhou classics and to strenuously suppressing their desires. Finally, it mocks those who practiced "guiding and pulling" exercises that often entailed imitating animals, accusing them of cultivating their bodies rather than their minds, and those who blindly

---

58 Huang, *A Walk in the Night with Zhuangzi: Musings on an Ancient Chinese Manuscript* (Albany: SUNY Press, 2023).

59 On its deriving a theory of rulership from the *Laozi* and the *Zhuangzi*, see Kanaya Osamu 金谷治, *Rō-Sō-teki sekai: Enanji no shisō* 老莊的世界:淮南子の思想 (Kyoto: Heirakuji Shoten, 1963), pp. 121–252. On *qi*, the body, and politics, see Hiraoka Teikichi 平岡禎吉, *Enanji ni arwareta ki no kenkyū* 淮南子に現れた氣の研究 (Tokyo: Kangi Bunka Gakkai, 1961). For a study of ch. 7, see Claude Larre, *Le Traité VII du Houai Nan Tseu* (Taipei: Instituts Ricci, 1982).

60 *Huainanzi* 淮南子, annotated by Gao You 高誘, in *Xin bian zhuzi ji cheng*, vol. 7 (Taipei: Shijie, 1974), ch. 7, pp. 99–100. The sage's stilling of his senses, as well as letting go of his limbs, are also discussed in ch. 6, p. 97.

pursued extending life through moxibustion and acupuncture.[61] This shows how the various styles of cultivating the embodied self had begun to engage in polemics by early empires.

Nourishing the Embodied Self through Hygienic Culture

In the same period that the philosophical masters increasingly focused on perfecting the body and its energies, masters of specialized disciplines did likewise. The most important of these were healers (*yi* 醫), who as will be discussed below gradually came to be defined as masters of a technical discipline that rigorously theorized a newly *medicalized* body, but several other types of specialists also discussed perfecting the embodied self. Among the earliest texts citing such men was the *Zuo zhuan*.

The *Zuo zhuan* contains anecdotes which portray conflicts in explaining the cause of a ruler's disease between technical specialists – diviners and a healer – and a philosophically inclined political actor and generalist, Zichan. In one story diviners sought the name of a spirit that caused the ruler's illness (see below) and obtained two names that they did not recognize. Zichan explained that they were the spirits of a star and a river, which could not cause a ruler's illness. Instead, this was due to his wastefully dispersing his *qi* energies, so they become blocked and thereby weakened his body. He also argued that the disease resulted from his having women of his own surname in the harem.[62] The ruler rewarded Zichan, but summoned a healer from Qin for a second opinion. The latter offered a variation of Zichan's explanation, suggesting that the disease resulted from sexual excess, and elaborated his diagnosis with an account of *qi* as a cosmic force that produced the four seasons, as well as such phenomena as wind, rain, dark, and light. The ruler praised Zichan as a "true gentleman broadly versed in things," and doubled his parting gift, while a minister praised the healer as "a fine healer."[63] Both figures are praised, but the distinction between them is clear.

---

[61] For accounts of the Perfected People, their conduct, and attributes, see *Huainanzi*, ch. 7, pp. 101, 103, 104–105, 107, 107–108, 111. On the images from the *Zhuangzi* and techniques of the heart-mind, see pp. 103–104. For the denunciation of shallow scholars, see pp. 110–111. For the mockery of exercises and medical therapies, see pp. 102, 105. Ch. 9 on "The Techniques of the Ruler" also discusses how the ruler develops his power through cultivating his bodily energies, above all his spirit. See pp. 127 (the Divine Husbandman transformed his people like a spirit, without using laws or punishments), 129 (spirit transformation is the noblest, and perfected essence [*zhi jing*] becomes spirit), 130 [3] (his perfected essence is like the life-giving of spring *qi* and the killing of autumn *qi*; the perfected essence of the sage-kings took form within them; the loftiest form of rule is spirit transformation), 134 (the Way of the ruler endlessly transforms like a spirit), 138, 139.

[62] *Zuo zhuan zhu*, Zhao 1, pp. 1219, 1220–1221.

[63] *Zuo zhuan zhu*, Zhao 1, pp. 1221–1222. The doctor also explains the disease as a form of *gu*, a disease discussed in Paul Unschuld, *Medicine in China: A History of Ideas* (Berkeley: University of California Press, 1985), pp. 46–50; Harper, *Early Chinese Medical Literature*,

The earlier story of using divination to identify the spirits who caused a disease – and establishing what sacrifice should be offered to that spirit to make it desist – continued a practice observed in the Shang oracle inscriptions of assigning the causes of disease to invasive powers and treating them with sacrifice or exorcism. The endurance into the late fourth century BCE of this pattern of diagnosing and treating diseases is also demonstrated by contents of the tomb of Shao Tuo, a high official of Chu state who was buried in 316. His tomb contained a record of turtle and milfoil divinations performed on his behalf, and the last six dealt with attempts to identify the spirit(s) causing his heart problems, and the ritual procedures to assuage them.[64] These records and related documents in the tomb reveal how the conduct of the Chu elite, and their understanding of the protection and cultivation of their bodies, depended on guidance from spiritual technicians. From other tombs we know that at this time diagnosis and therapy were increasingly shaped by theories of *yin* and *yang*, and of hemerological calendars that derived diagnosis and treatment from "almanacs" of auspicious and inauspicious days. However, the *Lü shi chun qiu* states that the old pattern, which it criticized, was still the most common well into the third century BCE.[65]

Although the Baoshan tomb suggests conservatism in explaining diseases and their treatment, it also had new features which were part of a transformation of the understanding of the dead and their relation to the living. Constance Cook has used the texts and material remains in the tomb to work out how illness and death were viewed as steps in a spiritual journey from one realm to another.[66] This journey expresses new ideas about the nature of death, for it invokes evolving naturalistic laws based on a ritual calendar that cites the directions, the seasons, and the emerging systems of cosmic phases of elements and energies. In this process the grave became a liminal space from which the deceased departed toward the northwest to join a bureaucratically structured community. In addition to the divination records, the texts included an inventory of goods in the tomb which was read as a part of a ceremony of separating the dead from the living. Thus, this funerary ritual aimed at the creation and

pp. 74–75, 158–159, 300–302. For a critical discussion of the *Zuo zhuan*'s presentation of this case, see Miranda Brown, *The Art of Medicine in Early China: The Ancient and Medieval Origins of a Modern Archive* (Cambridge: Cambridge University Press, 2015), ch. 1, pp. 21–40.

64 Harper, "Iatromancy, Diagnosis, and Prognosis in Early Chinese Medicine," in *Innovation in Chinese Medicine*, ed. Elizabeth Hsu (Cambridge: Cambridge University Press, 2001), pp. 103–106. Evidence on healing from excavated texts is synthesized in Cook, *Medicine and Healing in Ancient East Asia*.

65 On the emerging, calendrical theories, see Harper, "Iatromancy, Diagnosis and Prognosis," pp. 107–119. On the flourishing of the old practices in the third century, see Chen Qiyou 陳奇猷, *Lü shi qun qiu jiaoshi* 呂氏春秋校釋 (Shanghai: Xuelin, 1984), ch. 3, p. 137.

66 Constance Cook, *Death in Ancient China: The Tale of One Man's Journey* (Leiden: Brill, 2006).

conveyance of a new type of post-mortem being who no longer settled into the collective status of ancestors defined by their place in the lineage.

These features of this and related Chu tombs from the same period are further elaborated in Lai Guolong's *Excavating the Afterlife*.[67] He works out changes that characterized mortuary ritual in the late Warring States, most notably this shift from merging the deceased with collective, benevolent ancestors to creating or transforming an individual who moved in a controlled process through the realm of the dead. Second, the spirits invoked in the divinations as potential causes of his illness are no longer primarily ancestors, as in the Shang, but nature deities or people who died without ancestors, died violently, or drowned. These spirits, whom Lai calls "the dead who would not be ancestors," suggest the violence and social instability that marked the Warring States, but they are also a key step in the transition in the period toward the belief that the dead were dangerous spirits, and that funerary ritual served primarily to separate them from the living. The idea that violent death was a bad death that blocked becoming an ancestor, the elaboration of more detailed models of the body and the soul within funerary ritual, and the emergence of a more detailed afterlife for the deceased all contributed to a new focus in funerary ritual on forming a distinctive, posthumous self.[68]

In addition to this use of mortuary ritual to create and guide a new type of self through its posthumous existence, discoveries from the late Warring States and the early Han have also revealed many medical theories and procedures that greatly differ from the later physician-centered world of the *Huangdi neijing* (see below). Most important is the collection of medical manuscripts found in tomb 3 at Mawangdui, as well as related documents found in a tomb dating to the same period at Zhangjiashan.[69] These texts, conventionally treated as examples of the "nourishing life" (養生 *yang sheng*) theories of the late Warring States, include discussions of bodily vessel channels (脈 *mai*) and their *qi* energies, recipes for drugs and exorcisms,

---

[67] Guolong Lai, *Excavating the Afterlife: The Archaeology of Early Chinese Religion* (Seattle: University of Washington Press, 2015).

[68] On the shift from the dead as largely protective ancestors to dangerous individuals, see also Lewis, *The Construction of Space*, pp. 59–61, 121–129. For a parallel study arguing for a shift from personhood constructed through kinship and hereditary status to the self as an achieved construction, see Martin Powers, *Pattern and Person: Ornament, Society, and Self in Classical China* (Cambridge, Mass.: Harvard University Press, 2006). On the enduring belief that violent death was a "bad" death that produced an evil spirit unless the deceased was given offerings (in imperial China through "deification"), see Brigitte Baptandier, *De la malemort en quelques pays d'Asie* (Paris: Karthala, 2001).

[69] Ma Jixing 馬繼興, *Mawangdui gu yishu kaoshi* 馬王堆古醫書考釋 (Changsha: Hunan Kexue Jishu Chubanshe, 1992); Harper, *Early Chinese Medical Literature; Zhangjiashan Han mu zhu jian* 張家山漢墓竹簡 (Beijing: Wenwu Chubanshe, 2001), pp. 75–80, 109–118, 235–246, 285–299.

breath cultivation, sexual techniques, and dietetics. As Donald Harper has argued, the placement of these texts in tombs, and the nature of their contents, suggest that they circulated among educated members of the elite who were not trained physicians, but rather amateurs who hoped to improve their own bodies and extend their life spans. Only the texts on channels and therapy through moxibustion (in contrast to the later *Huangdi neijing*, acupuncture is never mentioned) assume the work of a physician, and only one mentions students receiving instruction from a master.[70]

This suggests a world in the late fourth through the first century BCE where ideas about therapies for body and spirit could be divided into four currents. First, there was the philosophical tradition stemming from "Inner Training" in which the meditative production of a perfected mind and body led to the inward gathering and then outward projection of refined energies or spirit to create social order. Second, the *Zhuangzi* referred to ideas, linked to the *xian* cult in the third century, for creating an ethereal spirit-body which could soar through the Heavens. Third, there were the techniques described in the texts from Mawangdui and Zhangjiashan in which elite men used hygienic techniques of breathing, stretching, sexual cultivation, and recipes to improve their health and extend longevity. Finally, as will be discussed below, there were methods for diagnosis and therapy, in part derived from religion and magic but increasingly based on theories of nature, through which trained physicians could diagnose and treat their patients. Below, I briefly sketch the hygienic practices for self-treating elite men. Following Harper, I place the discussion under four rubrics – breath cultivation, exercises, sexual cultivation, and dietetics – while noting that these four all focus on the ingestion and circulation of fresher *qi* energies.[71]

The earliest reference to a breathing exercise to extend life appears in a set of nine rhyming, trisyllabic phrases placed under the rubric "circulating *qi*" (*xing qi* 行氣) on a dodecagonal block of jade probably carved in the late fourth or early third century BCE.[72] In using verse, presumably to be recited as an epitome of more detailed instructions received from a master, it hints at influence from the "Inner Training" or the *Laozi*, but does not provide enough detail to be studied in isolation. However, it argues that *qi* should first flow downward

70 Harper, *Early Chinese Medical Literature*, pp. 36–38, 42–45, 55–57, 142–147. The reference to master-disciple transmission is noted on p. 55. The translation of the original is on pp. 217–218 (Ma, *Mawangdui*, pp. 302–303).

71 Harper, *Early Chinese Medical Texts*, "Techniques" (pp. 125–142).

72 Li Ling 李零, *Zhongguo fangshu kao* 中國方術考 (Beijing: Renmin Zhongguo Chubanshe, 1983), pp. 320–323.

and, after transformation, return upward, anticipating the later "Model of the Vessels [*mai fa* 脈法]" from Mawangdui.[73]

In contrast with the jade, the Mawangdui texts on breathing exercises, especially "Eliminating Grain and Consuming *Qi* [*que gu shi qi*却穀食氣]" and sections from the "Ten Questions [*shi wen* 十問]," give more detailed instructions, although sometimes in a metaphorical language.[74] The purpose of this esoteric style is uncertain, but it might render the act more spiritual or give it a cosmic aspect. The texts also espouse a regimen of breathing exercises that vary through the seasons and are mapped onto the time of day, most commonly entailing expelling old energies at night and inhaling new ones in the morning. Other sections describe how the ingested energies can be directed to designated spots in the body, such as the chest or the four extremities. The discussion in the first of the "Ten Questions" presents a lengthy process of compressing and transmuting the inhaled *qi* energies, then spreading them to the flesh, skin, and tips of the hair, all as a preliminary to eating.

The second major aspect, exercises, is generally discussed under the rubric of "pulling" (*yin* 引) or "guiding and pulling" (*dao yin* 導引). The latter term apparently refers to both "breathing" (*dao* as guiding the *qi*) and exercise, and accounts of exercise routines in the *Book of Exercises* (*yin shu*) from Zhangjiashan almost all discuss how the breath is to be associated with the physical exercises.[75] In contrast with exercise routines in the early West, which aimed at developing a large, articulated musculature, these exercises were intended to maximize flexibility and the movement of *qi* through the body. This contrast reflects a significant distinction in how the structures of the body were articulated in the two cultures.[76] The *Exercises* begins with a series of routines associated sequentially with spring, summer, autumn, and winter, and others follow the time of day. It includes both accounts of individual exercises, for example, "pulling yin," which is basically a toe-touch, with more elaborate sequences to achieve specific purposes, such as treating a stipulated ailment.

---

[73] Harper, *Early Chinese Medical Literature*, pp. 213–214; Ma, *Mawangdui*, pp. 276, 282.

[74] Harper, *Early Chinese Medical Literature*, pp. 305–309, 385–388, 393–399, 409–411; Ma, *Mawangdui*, pp. 822–846, 867–876, 897–932, 967–972. The linked practices of eschewing grain while engaging in breathing exercises to create a lighter body also figure in the biography of Zhang Liang, an adviser of the Han founder. See *Shi ji* 史記, by Sima Qian 司馬遷 (d. 86 BCE) and Sima Tan 司馬談 (165–110 BCE) (Beijing: Zhonghua, 1959), ch. 55, p. 2048. His practice, however, is linked to the *xian* cult, as he is said to "want to follow [the immortal] Master Red Pine."

[75] See Gao Dalun 高大倫, *Zhangjiashan Han Jian "Yin Shu" Yanjiu* 張家山漢簡"引書"研究 (Changdu: Ba Shu Shushe, 1995), which precedes an annotated version of the text with a detailed analysis of its ideas and relations to other texts.

[76] See Kuriyama, *Expressiveness of the Body*, ch. 3, "Muscularity and Identity," as well as Figures 1–2 on pp. 10–11. The entire book elaborates this contrast.

It concludes with a list of exercises identified by what part of the body or physiological function they benefit.[77]

In addition to dealing with breathing, some of the exercise routines also incorporate dietetics as a means of ingesting *qi*. Thus the exercise named "increasing *yin* energies" (*yi yin qi* 益陰氣) stipulates that it cannot be performed at the end of the month (when the *yin* is at its peak), describes a posture to be assumed, and then prescribes:

> Take cooked grain in your right hand and hold it over the mouth. Then inhale the *qi* of the grain, doing this to the utmost. Then eat it. Press down both thighs, bend the waist, and extend the lesser abdomen forward, using your force to the utmost. Do not drink or swallow saliva. Repeat twice and stop after this third time.[78]

This exercise, which is mapped onto the time of the month, entails physical stretching, breathing cultivation (entailed in the "utmost" inhalation of the grain's *qi*), and eating. Several other exercises also prescribe "pulling the buttocks" (*yin kao* 引尻), that is, constricting the anus.[79] This would propel *qi* energies that were being forcefully compressed in the lesser abdomen, and was a frequent aspect of sexual cultivation exercises.

Before discussing such exercises, we should note that the Mawangdui texts include one with forty-four drawings of *daoyin* exercises. Unfortunately, their captions are largely lost and the drawings depict only static poses which thus exclude the dynamic series described in the Zhangjiashan *Exercises Book*.[80] However, many of the titles of the illustrations indicate that the exercises entailed animal imitation, such as the "bear ramble," and this also figures in the *Exercises Book*.[81] Clearly animals exemplified distinctive types of force or energy, so that imitating them could improve people's bodies. This resembles texts on longevity that advocated imitating the breathing of turtles or other long-lived creatures. Two discussions of the sage's model for cultivating sex also list animal imitations.[82]

Sexual cultivation was the focus of two Mawangdui texts, and references to it were scattered through others, especially the recipe books on "nurturing life"

---

77 Gao, *"Yin Shu" Yanjiu*, pp. 90–97, 129.

78 Gao, *"Yin Shu" Yanjiu*, p. 134. Combining exercise with eating is also described in Mawangdui's "Recipes for Nurturing Life [*yang sheng fang* 養生方]." See Harper, *Early Chinese Medical Literature*, p. 359; Ma, *Mawangdui*, p. 746.

79 Gao, *"Yin Shu" Yanjiu*, p. 145.

80 Harper, *Early Chinese Medical Literature*, pp. 310–327; Ma, *Mawangdui*, pp. 849–866.

81 Gao, *"Yin Shu" Yanjiu*, pp. 103, 104, 107, 112, 113, 115, 131, 141.

82 Harper, *Early Chinese Medical Literature*, pp. 356–357, 432; Ma, *Mawangdui*, pp. 740–743, 1047–1048. See Lisa Raphals, "Human and Animal in China and Greece," in *Ancient Greece and China Compared*, ed. G. E. R. Lloyd and J. J. Zhao (Cambridge: Cambridge University Press, 2018), pp. 131–159.

and "various cures."[83] The two texts that focused on sexual cultivation rely on elements of verse, with extensive rhymed passages, as well as frequent metaphors and phonetic echoes that provide esoteric terms for parts of the female body, or map that body onto world geography. Thus, they exhibit lingering influences of the philosophical writings on perfecting the self, such as "Inner Training," the *Laozi*, and the *Han Feizi*, which also used verse to suggest the loftiness of the subject and to facilitate memorization.[84] While one passage warns of the dangers of excessive lust, which the sage avoided through establishing models for intercourse (which elsewhere include animal imitations), the Mawangdui texts differ from the most common discussions of sex. These warn against excessive sexual activity (like the physician and Zichan in the *Zuo zhuan*), use intercourse as a metaphor for key human relations such as that between the ruler and his ministers, or (in later times) treat intercourse as a vampiric combat where each party seeks to extract the other's energies through inducing an orgasm while oneself refraining.[85]

To summarize their teachings, the texts treat sexual cultivation as a means of generating energies and essence (*jing*) which create a lighter, more refined body that approaches the condition of a spirit (*shen*). Although some passages

---

[83] Harper, "Conjoining Yin and Yang (*he yin yang* 合陰陽)," *Early Chinese Medical Literature*, pp. 412–422; "Discussion of the Supreme Way under Heaven [*tianxia zhi dao tan* 天下至道談]," pp. 425–438; Ma, *Mawangdui*, pp. 977–1011, 1012–1072; Donald Harper, "The Sexual Arts of Ancient China as Described in a Manuscript of the Second Century B.C." *Harvard Journal of Asiatic Studies* 47.2 (1987): 539–592; Rudolph Pfister, *Der beste Weg unter dem Himmel: Sexuelle Körpertechniken aus dem altem China; Zwei Bambustexte aus Mawangdui* (Zürich: Museum Rietberg, 2003). The third of the "Ten Questions" describes "conjoining *qi*" to revitalize an aged man and prolong his life. The sixth question discusses a breathing exercise that revitalizes the penis. The eighth question describes how exercise and eating allowed Yu to revitalize himself and satisfy his queen. See Harper, *Literature*, pp. 389–391, 400–401, 404–406; Ma, *Mawangdui*, pp. 888–892, 914, 923–925, 940–947.

[84] Gundula Linck, "Der poetische Körper von Mawangdui: Texte zur Lebenspflege aus dem 2. Jahrhundert v. Chr," in *Han-Zeit: Festschrift für Hans Stumpfeldt aus Anlass seines 65. Geburtstages*, ed. Michael Friedrich, Reinhard Emmerich, and Hans van Ess, *Lun Wen: Studien zur Geistesgeschichte und Literatur in China* 8 (Wiesbaden: Harrasowitz, 2008), pp. 11–25. On self-care in later Chinese verse, see Fang Chunyang 方春陽, ed., *Zhongguo yangsheng dacheng* 中國養生大成 (Jilin: Jilin Kexue Jishu Chubanshe, 1992); Li Yuanguo 李遠國, ed., *Qigong jing hua ji* 氣功精華集 (Chengdu: Zhonghua Chuantong Yangsheng Congshu, 1988), pp. 138–162.

[85] The warning about the problem of lust is in the "Supreme Way" text. See Harper, *Literature*, p. 432; Ma, *Mawangdui*, p. 1046. For a discussion of the use in early China of sexual union as an image for key human relations, see Paul Rakita Goldin, *The Culture of Sex in Ancient China* (Honolulu: University of Hawai'i Press, 2002), esp. ch. 1, which discusses how commentaries read early poetry on romance and sex as allegories of politics. On how poems celebrated the king's sexual union with a goddess as a figure for winning control of the land, see Paul Rouzer, *Articulated Ladies: Gender and the Male Community in Early Chinese Texts* (Cambridge, Mass.: Harvard University Press, 2001), ch. 2. On later ideas of sex as a battle for energies, with a brief discussion of the Mawangdui texts, see Douglas Wile, *Art of the Bedchamber: The Chinese Sexual Yoga Classics Including Women's Solo Meditation Texts* (Albany: SUNY Press, 1992).

discuss the woman's pleasure (in "conjoining yin and yang" she must achieve orgasm), indicate that she can physically benefit, and stipulate that the man must not "control," the focus is on him. The texts break down the act of sex, which it labels the "Way of play/enjoyment" (*xi dao* 戲道), into a series of steps: foreplay, sexual positions, signs of female arousal, the art of using the penis, and the culminating moment of female orgasm. There is some discussion of avoiding premature ejaculation, but it is unclear whether the male should ideally achieve an orgasm. The sequence is also numerically analyzed: "ten positions" that could be assumed (identified as *shi* 勢, a military-political term for "fluid power of circumstances," most of which entail animal imitation), "five signs" of a woman's approaching climax, "ten movements" to be made by the penis, and "nine manners" to thrust it. In the account of the "ten movements" of the penis, each step is marked by a bodily transformation resembling those attained in meditation: the eyes and ears becoming perceptive, the voice becoming brilliant, the skin glowing, the muscles growing strong, and ultimately attaining the ideal state of "spirit illumination" (*shen ming*).[86]

While the sexual chapters do not discuss the questions of frequency or the number of partners, one section in "Recipes for Nurturing Life [*yang sheng fang* 養生方]" discusses substances that could be eaten that allowed a man to have sex with multiple partners.[87] Several modern scholars have also suggested that the emphasis in the sexual-cultivation texts on stroking or pressing zones of the body that produced distant responses could well have provided a model for the idea of a body structured by channels where therapy by moxibustion or acupuncture likewise influenced at a distance.[88]

As for dietetics, the recipe chapters describe drugs, beverages, and foods that can supplement the diet and prepare for exercises or meals, and they do not stipulate the ascetic program of grain elimination. They do, however, describe many plants and other natural substances, as well as the methods of processing them, including magical incantations.[89] There are formulae in "Recipes for Nurturing Life" for treating inability to achieve erections (sometimes due to age), increasing the size or pliancy of the erect penis, stimulating the man's sexual excitement, increasing the

86 Both major texts on sexual cultivation discuss using sex to transform the body and achieve spirit illumination. See Harper, *Early Chinese Medical Literature*, pp. 418, 427; Ma, *Mawangdui*, pp. 989, 1025.

87 Harper, *Early Chinese Medical Literature*, pp. 135–140.

88 See, for example, Vivienne Lo, "The Influence of Nurturing Life Culture on the Development of Western Han Acumoxa Therapy," in *Innovation in Chinese Medicine*, ed. Elisabeth Hsu (Cambridge: Cambridge University Press, 2001), pp. 39–47.

89 On the development of pharmaceutical theory and practice in the later Chinese *ben cao* 本草 tradition, see Paul Unschuld, *Medicine in China: A History of Pharmaceuticals* (Berkeley: University of California Press, 1986); Vivienne Lo, "Pleasure, Prohibition and Pain: Food and Medicine in China," in *Of Tripod and Palate*, pp. 163–186.

woman's sexual desire, removing the woman's body hairs, treating genital swelling, or facilitating sexual intercourse.[90] Sexual treatments are also scattered through the "Recipes for Various Cures [*za liao fang* 雜療方]."[91]

Other texts on recipes, for example, "Recipes for Fifty-two Ailments [*wushier bing fang* 五十二病方]," aim at treating diseases and pains or working magic for such ends as eliminating marital hostility, seducing a noble, dispelling bad dreams, preventing mothers-in-law and wives from fighting, stopping infants from crying, and winning lawsuits ["Recipes for Various Charms"].[92] Given the celebration of the skilled physician's ability to foresee and forestall diseases before they are even perceived by the patient, this emphasis on treating diseases that have already developed and on dealing with existing failures in sexual performance suggests that recipes are in some way secondary or inferior to the interlinked program of breathing, exercise, and controlled sex traced out above. The "Discussion of the Supreme Way Under Heaven" supports this idea in stating that if the man "impulsively" (*ji* 疾, which as a noun means "illness") has sex without proper preparation and control, he will fall ill from disordered *qi* and consequent "inner fevers." These must then be treated with medicine, moxibustion, and diet to "bolster his exterior" (*fu qi wai* 輔其外).[93] Using medicine and dietetics to treat an "exterior" that has fallen ill due to an "interior" disturbed by failure in self-control demonstrates the relative status of the two approaches to bodily health.

A final set of medical texts from Mawangdui, and a related example from Zhangjiashan, provide an early account of the vessels through which *qi* moved as a new model of the body, theory of illness, and form of therapy.[94] The model of the body where *qi* and blood flow through channels was first mentioned in a text

---

90 Harper, *Early Chinese Medical Literature*, pp. 328–344, 348, 355–358; Ma, *Mawangdui*, pp. 653–705, 718, 739–745. This last section describes "conjoining *qi*" (*he qi* 合氣) with young women as patterned on the sage-king Yu's intercourse with his wives, a practice which rejuvenates an older man. Rejuvenation through sexual cultivation recurs elsewhere, as in Harper, *Literature*, p. 428; Ma, *Mawangdui*, p. 1030.

91 Harper, *Early Chinese Medical Literature*, pp. 363–371; Ma, *Mawangdui*, pp. 749–778.

92 Harper, *Early Chinese Medical Literature*, pp. 221–304, 423–424; Ma, *Mawangdui*, pp. 323–644, 1006–1011. On disease-curing recipes, see also Harper, *The "Wu Shih Erh Ping Fang": Translation and Prolegomena*, Ph.D. dissertation, University of California at Berkeley (Ann Arbor: University Microfilms, 1982). On magical practices in early China and their relation to self-therapy and medicine, see Harper, *Early Chinese Medical Literature*, pp. 69–74, 95–96, 103–104, 148–183. On the Mawangdui texts indicating a transition between a magical worldview and a naturalist theory of correspondences, both of which survived and evolved over the centuries, see Linck, "Der poetische Körper," pp. 13–14.

93 Harper, *Early Chinese Medical Literature*, p. 429; Ma, *Mawangdui*, p. 1032.

94 Harper, *Early Chinese Medical Literature*, pp. 192–220; Ma, *Mawangdui*, pp. 173–311; "Mai shu 脈書," *Zhangjiashan Han mu zhu jian*, pp. 235–246. On evolving ideas about the vessels, see Paul U. Unschuld, *Huang Di Nei Jing Su Wen: Nature, Knowledge, Imagery in an Ancient Chinese Medical Text* (Berkeley: University of California Press, 2003), pp. 167–180.

on water (probably fourth century BCE) preserved in the *Guanzi*: "Water is blood and vapor of the earth, like what flows through the muscles and vessels."[95] The Mawangdui texts have developed a more detailed model which traces eleven yin and yang channels, primarily along the legs and arms.[96] The origins of this idea of vessels running through the body is uncertain, although blood vessels are an obvious model, and the above passage suggests that muscles might also have contributed, as do body-earth correspondences, with vessels acting like streams. The fact that stroking and pressing in sexual foreplay elicited physical responses at a distance may also have supported the idea. While this model moved towards that expounded later in the Yellow Emperor corpus (with identical names for many channels), it differs in having only eleven vessels (rather than twelve), in not linking the vessels into a body-wide circulatory system, and in arguing that the yin energies in the yin vessels are identified with death. This last point has been invoked to explain why a black lacquer figurine discovered in Mianyang, Sichuan in 1993 traces the lines of the vessels in red, but omits the yin vessels, thus suggesting a perfected body.[97]

In addition to indicating an emergent model of the body, the texts on vessels also present a new idea of disease. Earlier accounts of the origins of disease, as in Shang divination records and the Baoshan texts, identified ailments as spirits attacking the body, and therapy consisted of identifying the attackers to be able to assuage or exorcise them. In the vessel texts, health depended on maintaining the proper flow of blood and *qi*, and diseases were explained as some functional failure, such as flowing in the wrong direction or stagnating. Consequently, therapy consisted in restoring harmony and proper flow within the body, which is itself the cause of the disease and indeed the disease itself.[98] Harper, citing

---

95 *Guanzi jiao zhu*, ch. 14, "Shui di 水地," p. 813. Another essay preserved in this text describes "guiding" (*dao*, the same term applied to exercises in the Mawangdui texts) the "blood and *qi*" to "constitute the embodied self" (*wei shen* 為身, in parallel to "constituting the state") to prolong bodily existence. See ch. 19, "Zhong kuang 中匡," pp. 385–386. The "Inner Training" refers to the blood and *qi* being tranquil when the four limbs are correctly placed. See ch. 16, p. 943. Ch. 17, "Jin zang 禁葬," p. 1012 refers to "food and drink being sufficient to harmonize the blood and *qi*." Thus, these texts already invoked both exercises and diet. On ideas about "blood and *qi*," see Unschuld, *Huang Di Nei Jing Su Wen*, pp. 144–167.

96 Yamada Keiji has suggested that the priority of the foot/leg vessels resulted from the emphasis on *qi* moving up or down. See Yamada Keiji 山田慶兒, "Maōtai Kan bo shutsudo isho sansoku 馬王堆漢墓出土醫書三則," in *Shin hatsugen Chūgoku kagakushi shiryō no kenkyū* 新發現中國科學史資料の研究, ed. Yamada, 2 vols. (Kyoto: Kyōto Daigaku Jinbun Kagaku Kenkyūsho, 1985), p. 69. See also Yamada, "The Formation of the *Huang-ti Nei-ching*," *Acta Asiatica* 36 (1979): 67–89.

97 See He Zhiguo and Vivienne Lo, "The Channels: A Preliminary Examination of a Lacquered Figurine from the Western Han Period," *Early China* 21 (1996): 81–123. On this explanation for the absence of yin vessels, see pp. 112–116.

98 On the idea in ancient Greece of the disordered body itself as the disease, see Maria Michela Sassi, *The Science of Man in Ancient Greece*, tr. Paul Tucker (Chicago: University of Chicago

earlier works by Paul Unschuld, distinguishes these two models as "ontological" (disease as a thing) and "functional" or "physiological" (disease as a disturbance in correct action).[99] Whereas most diseases in the recipes texts, particularly the "Recipes for Fifty-Two Ailments," are still externally caused, the vessel texts explain diseases through failed or improper energy flows.

This shift in explaining the origins of ailments also changed how they were named and classified. Whereas the "ontological" diseases were named for the outside entity that produced them, accounts of diseases due to vessels largely named them through their location. In the Mawangdui texts this consists largely of speaking of pain (or numbness or cold) located in certain parts of the body. The "Vessel Book [*mai shu* 脈書]" found at Zhangjiashan is even more systematic, listing possible locations for ailments and giving each ailment a name depending on that location.[100] A later passage in the same text, which has no parallel in the Mawangdui texts, divides the body into "six constituents" – bones, muscles, blood, vessels, flesh, and *qi* – describes the type of pain produced by ailments in each constituent, and argues that the entire body would collapse through failure to identify these pains. This extends the signaling function of pain that figures in all the vessel texts into a more general theory of pain as the chief identifier of disease.[101] It also suggests that part of the motivation for shifting toward the new

Press, 2001), ch. 4; Brooke Holmes, *The Symptom and the Subject: The Emergence of the Physical Body in Ancient Greece* (Princeton: Princeton University Press, 2010), ch. 2–4.

99 Unschuld, "Traditional Chinese Medicine: Some Historical and Epistemological Reflections," *Social Science and Medicine* 24 (1987): 1023–1029; " History of Chinese Medicine," in *The Cambridge World History of Human Disease*, ed. Kenneth F. Kiple (Cambridge: Cambridge University Press, 1993), pp. 20–27; Robert P. Hudson, "Concepts of Disease in the West," in *The Cambridge World History of Human Disease*, pp. 45–52; Emiko Ohnuki-Tierney, *Illness and Healing among the Sakhalin Ainu: A Symbolic Interpretation* (Cambridge: Cambridge University Press, 1981), ch. 6–7; *Good, Medicine, Rationality, and Experience*, ch. 2–3.

100 *Zhangjiashan Han mu zhu jian*, p. 235.

101 *Zhangjiashan Han mu zhu jian*, p. 244; Vivienne Lo, "Tracking the Pain: *Jue* and the Formation of a Theory of Circulating *Qi* through the Channels," *Sudhoffs Archiv* 83.2 (1999): 191–211. A more systematic study of ideas about pain in early China would allow comparisons with the substantial literature on the cultural history of ideas about pain in European languages, including Thomas Dormandy, *The Worst of Evils: The Fight against Pain* (New Haven: Yale University Press, 2006); Roselyne Rey, *Histoire de la douleur* (Paris: La Découverte, 1993); Elaine Scarry, *The Body in Pain: The Making and Unmaking of the World* (Oxford: Oxford University Press, 1985); David B. Morris, *The Culture of Pain* (Berkeley: University of California Press, 1991); Valerie Gray Hardcastle, *The Myth of Pain* (Cambridge, Mass.: MIT Press, 1999); Ariel Glucklich, *Sacred Pain: Hurting the Body for the Sake of the Soul* (Oxford: Oxford University Press, 2001); Rainer-M. E. Jacobi, ed., *Schmerz und Sprache: Zur medizinischen Anthropologie Viktor von Weizsäckers* (Heidelberg: Universitätsverlag, 2012); Hans-Georg Gadamer, *Schmerz: Einschätzungen aus medizinischer, philosophischer und therapeutischer Sicht* (Heidelberg: Universitätsverlag, 2010); Frederik Buytendijk, *Pain*, tr. Eda O'Shiel (Westport: Greenwood Press, 1961); David Bakan, *Disease, Pain, and Sacrifice: Toward a Psychology of Suffering* (Chicago: University of Chicago Press, 1968); Margaret Abruzzo, *Polemical Pain: Slavery, Cruelty, and the Rise of Humanitarianism* (Baltimore: The Johns Hopkins University Press,

model was that it established a hierarchy of bodily constituents moving from the heaviest and most solid to the lightest and most ethereal. Recalling that exercises and diet served largely to produce lighter and more refined substances (from *qi* to *jing* to *shen or shenming*) within the body, and that the "Inner Training" sought to empty the body to draw in refined substances, we can see a model in which treating diseases was a lower stage in a more general transformation of the body into a refined and ethereal being. The lacquered figurine from Mianyang also suggests this model of bodily transformation.[102]

The vessel texts' model for treating diseases also indicates this shift toward combining therapy with seeking bodily perfection. Whereas the "ontological" diseases were treated with sacrifices, exorcisms, or ingesting recipe concoctions, the vessel texts base their treatments, which aim to restore proper flow of *qi*, on cauterization (or other means of applying heat) and lancing. The former was the preferred method, while the latter (still largely used for draining pus) was regarded as potentially dangerous and only used as a last resort. As Yamada Keiji has argued, the idea of applying heat, which would affect the condition of the *qi* within the vessels, predated the full-blown development of vessel-based therapy, and contributed to its elaboration.[103]

If cauterization failed to work, then the physician could resort to using a lancing-stone (*bian* 砭) to cut open a vessel at the elbow or knee to drain the *qi*, as modelled on draining pus. Stone itself had magical properties and was associated with the pursuit of the perfected body noted above. Moreover, the vivifying power of jade may have encouraged choosing it as the material substrate for the early inscription on circulating *qi*.[104] Nevertheless, such stones are most important as the immediate ancestor of the metal needles which began to be employed in the Han to perform acupuncture.[105]

2011); Thomas J. Csordas, *Embodiment and Experience: The Existential Ground of Culture and Self* (Cambridge: Cambridge University Press, 1994), Part IV.

102 Vivienne Lo, "The Han Period," in *Chinese Medicine and Healing: An Illustrated History*, ed. T. J. Hinrichs and Linda L. Barnes (Cambridge, Mass.: The Belknap Press of Harvard University Press, 2013), "Cultivating the Jade Body," pp. 49–51.

103 Yamada, "Shinkyū to tōeki no kigen 鍼灸と湯液の起源," in *Shin hatsugen Chūgoku kagakushi shiryō no kenkyū*, vol. 2, pp. 3–122; Yamada, *The Origins of Acupuncture, Moxibustion, and Decoction* (Kyoto: International Research Center for Japanese Studies, 1998); C. C. Epler, "Bloodletting in Early Chinese Medicine and Its Relation to the Origin of Acupuncture," *Bulletin of the History of Medicine* 54.3 (1980): 337–367.

104 Jade as a magical, life-endowing substance is often invoked to explain the jade suits in Han tombs. Moreover, its powers justified the belief that subterranean jade enabled mountains to produce clouds that bestowed life-giving rain. On the moisturizing, vivifying power of jade and some stones see *Huainanzi* 淮南子, in *Xin bian zhuzi ji cheng*, vol. 7 (Taipei: Shijie Shuju, 1974), ch. 2, pp. 22, 31, 32; ch. 4, p. 66 (this refers to yellow jade producing rain); ch. 14, p. 242; ch. 16, pp. 272 (jade in a mountain moistens the grasses and trees on it), 273.

105 On the therapeutic use of stones, see Vivienne Lo, "Lithic Therapy in Early Chinese Body Practices," in *Practitioners, Practices and Patients: New Approaches to Medical Archaeology*

One last cache of documents from the early Han, roughly contemporaneous with the texts from Mawangdui and Zhangjiashan, that sheds light on the transition from magical medicine and self-guided "nourishing life" to the physiological, acupuncture-based medicine of the Yellow Emperor corpus was the cases attributed to Chunyu Yi preserved in the *Shi ji*.[106] This man is described as master of the great granary of Qi, and was best known for a story in which his arrest led his daughter to appeal to the emperor to be made a female slave in his place, who was so moved that he decided to abolish mutilating punishments in 167 BCE. In that same year he summoned Chunyu Yi to court to ask why he treated ailments, and whom he had successfully treated (or accurately predicted the death, if they were beyond treatment). In response he described how he learned to diagnose and treat ailments, discussed twenty-five of his cases, and

and Anthropology, ed. P. A. Baker and G. Carr (Oxford: Oxbow Books, 2002), pp. 195–220; Lo, "Spirit of Stone: Technical Considerations in the Treatment of the Jade Body," *Bulletin of the School of Oriental and African Studies* 65 (2002): 99–128. A magical stone also figures in the story of Zhang Liang receiving his revealed military treatise from an old man who identifies himself as a transformation of a yellow stone. The Tang commentator Sima Zhen states that this stone was itself a transformation of Laozi, who was an incarnation of the Wind Monarch, a servant of the Yellow Emperor. See *Shi ji*, ch. 55, p. 2035. This story inspired the composition, probably in the late Western Han, of the politico-military treatise *Three Strategies of Lord Yellow Stone* (*huang shi gong san lüe* 黃石公三略). On its dating, see Ralph D. Sawyer, *The Seven Military Classics of Ancient China* (Boulder: Westview Press, 1993), pp. 281–284.

106 *Shi ji*, ch. 105, pp. 2794–2817. For a translation, see "Pien Ch'üeh and Ts'sang-kung, Memoir 45," tr. William H. Nienhauser and Elisabeth Hsu, in *The Grand Scribe's Records: Volume IX, the Memoirs of Han China, Part II, Ssu-ma Ch'ien* (Bloomington: Indiana University Press, 2011), pp. 1–88. On Chunyu Yi and the medical cases attributed to him, see Elizabeth Hsu, *Pulse Diagnosis in Early Chinese Medicine: The Telling Touch* (Cambridge: Cambridge University Press, 2010); Hsu, "Pulse Diagnostics in the Western Han: How *Mai* and *Qi* Determine *Bing*," in *Innovation in Chinese Medicine*, pp. 51–91; Miranda Brown, *The Art of Medicine in Early China*, pp. 63–86; Brown, "Looking Backward: The Rise of Medical Tradition in the Han Period," in *Chang'an 26 BCE: An Augustan Age in China*, ed. Michael Nylan and Griet Vankeerberghen (Seattle: University of Washington Press, 2015), pp. 441–460; Michael Loewe, "The Physician Chunyu Yi and His Historical Background," in *En suivant la voie royale: Mélanges en homage à Léon Verdermeersch*, ed. Jacques Gernet, Marc Kalinowski, and Jean-Pierre Dièny (Paris: École Française d''Extrême-Orient, 1997), pp. 195–220; Harper, *Early Chinese Medical Literature*, pp. 7–8, 45–46, 49, 55, 58–60, 67, 70–71, 73–78, 81–82, 91–95, 102.

On the significance of the case study and the narrative framing of illness in ancient China and elsewhere, see Christopher Cullen, "*Yi'an* 醫案 (Case Statements): The Origins of a Genre of Chinese Medical Literature," in *Innovation in Chinese Medicine*, pp. 297–323; Nathan Sivin, "Text and Experience in Classical Chinese Medicine," in *Knowledge and Scholarly Medical Traditions*, ed. Don Bates (Cambridge: Cambridge University Press, 1995), pp. 177–204; Charlotte Furth, Judith T. Zeitlin, and Ping-chen Hsiung, eds., *Thinking with Cases: Specialist Knowledge in Chinese Cultural History* (Honolulu: University of Hawai'i Press, 2007), Part 2; Arthur Kleinman, M. D., *The Illness Narratives: Suffering, Healing, and the Human Condition* (New York: Basic Books, 1988); *Good, Medicine, Rationality, and Experience*, ch. 3, 6; Kathryn Montgomery Hunter, *Doctors' Stories: The Narrative Structure of Medical Knowledge* (Princeton: Princeton University Press, 1991); Lawrence Rothfield, *Vital Signs: Medical Realism in Nineteenth-Century Fiction* (Princeton: Princeton University Press, 1992).

responded to eight official queries, in one of these more comprehensively narrating his studies.

While scholars have shown that there are anachronisms in some of his accounts, and argued that the twenty-five cases were probably conflated by Sima Qian from several documents, they *do* follow a standard pattern and evince a consistent approach to medicine.[107] To the extent that the cases were not forged by Sima Qian, an idea that no scholars endorse, this multiplicity of voices makes them even more valuable as evidence on ideas about healing that circulated among officials in the first century BCE. This also suggests that there were many men, like those buried at Mawangdui and Zhangjiashan, who were not professional physicians (to the extent that such a role existed at this time) but devoted time to studying healing. This idea is supported by materials cited by Miranda Brown, which show how diverse officials, military officers, an architect, and other people in this period treated various ailments.[108]

Chunyu Yi's account of his studies and cases indicates several things about treating disease in this period. First, as noted above, they show that diverse officials and other members of the elite had mastered sophisticated medical practices. In addition to the men from whom Chunyu Yi learned the arts of diagnosis and treating ailments, and the other implicit authors of cases, Yi lists several ordinary city dwellers, a couple officials, and even two Grand Physicians (*tai yi* 太醫) from a royal court who studied with him. He also lists the texts which he taught them, the length of their studies, and their degree of mastery.[109] This indicates some continuity with the medical culture suggested in the early Han tombs.

Second, the authors of the cases roughly agree on practice: privileging as the primary forms of diagnosis reading pulses as supplemented by examining the complexion, making predictions about the course of the disease, preferably treating them with a hot decoction, and resorting to stronger drugs and acupuncture or moxibustion as a last resort. Moreover, they follow a standard mode of presenting the case, which as Miranda Brown has suggested may be patterned on

[107] Jin Shiqi 金仕起, *Zhongguo gudai de yixue, yishi, yu zhengzhi: yi yishi wenben wei zhongxin de yige fenxi* 中國古代的醫學, 醫史與政治:以醫史文本為中心的一個分析 (Taipei: Zhengda Chubanshe, 2010), pp. 231–233; Loewe, "The Physician Chunyu Yi," p. 307; Hsu, *Pulse Diagnosis*, pp. 51–61; Brown, *The Art of Medicine*, pp. 78–79.

[108] Brown, *The Art of Medicine*, pp. 80–83. Many examples cited were collected in Xie Guihua, "Han Bamboo and Wooden Medical Records Discovered in Military Sites from the North-Western Frontier Regions," in *Medieval Chinese Medicine: The Dunhuang Medical Manuscripts*, ed. Christopher Cullen and Vivienne Lo (London: Routledge, 2005), pp. 77–106. For evidence from another region Brown also cites *Liye Qin Jiandu Jiaoshi* 里耶秦簡牘校釋 ed. Chen Wei 陳偉, He Youzu 何有祖, Lu Jialiang 魯家亮, and Fan Guodong 凡國棟 (Wuchang: Wuhan Daxue Chubanshe, 2012); *Liye Qin Jian* 里耶秦簡 (Beijing: Wenwu Chubanshe, 2012).

[109] *Shi ji*, ch. 105, pp. 2816–2817.

conventions in writing up legal cases. In each case they begin with an account of the background circumstances, including the title or status of the patient, their place of registration and name, and finally how the potential healer encountered them. They then provide a prognosis, usually after testing the pulse, describe how the ailment arose, and predict its course. Third, they often receive confirmation from the patient, who narrates a story that matches the healer's account of origins. Finally, they explain what characteristics of the pulse or the patient's complexion elicited their account of the disease's origins and course.

Third, a notable feature of his accounts of his studies (and to some degree of his teaching) is that they entail receiving esoteric texts from a master (Yang Qing or Gongsun Guang) who recognized Yi's remarkable character, selected him as heir to his texts, imposed a vow to never reveal the texts to others, either gave him the texts or orally presented them for transcription, and finally gave him lengthy instructions in using their teachings.[110] These themes of recognizing worth, disclosing efficacious texts, and imposing a vow of secrecy also figure in tales of the revelation of military texts, and scriptures in later religious Daoism. However, while emphasizing the transmission from a master, Chunyu Yi also insists that he does not know from whom Yang Qing received his texts, and the formulae from Gongsun Guang are simply described as "transmitted from ancient times," with no names of transmitters. Thus, there was no attempt to claim authority through establishing a medical lineage based on textual transmission. Indeed, the two men are described simply as the heads of wealthy households who studied these arts out of personal interest, without seeking to treat people.

Finally, in many cases the author refers to either a named medical practitioner or a collective "throng of healers" (*zhong yi* 眾醫) who invariably misdiagnose the case and often prescribe damaging therapies.[111] These recurring polemics, along with accounts of other texts on diagnosis and formulae which prove to be worthless, indicates a world marked by considerable competition between healers. It might also carry forward the tensions suggested in the *Zuo zhuan*'s account of medical attendant He and Zichan, in which the specialist and the learned official figure as rivals.

Healing the Embodied Self in the Yellow Emperor Corpus

The above account traced out a period from the late Warring States through the first century of the Western Han when diverse hygienic practices served to perfect and extend the body's powers, while assorted techniques of

[110] *Shi ji*, ch. 105, pp. 2794–2795, 2815–2816.

[111] *Shi ji*, ch. 105, pp. 2799, 2802, 2803, 2804, 2807, 2808, 2809, 2810, 2810–2811, 2811–2812, 2814–1815.

diagnosis and therapy were textually transmitted and studied by members of the elite, including government and military officials. Some of these texts were esoterically revealed in teacher-disciple transmissions, but this did not constitute medical lineages, they were not restricted to medical specialists or professional healers, and there was no overarching concept of "healing" (*yi* 醫) as a field of study. As argued by Miranda Brown, it seems that the definition of "medicine" as a coherent and independent discipline with a defined body of openly transmitted texts was first worked out by Liu Xiang (and his son Liu Xin) at the end of the Western Han. As bibliographer of the imperial text collection and leader of the classicizing movement that revived many early texts (such as the *Zuo zhuan*) or restored major texts that had fallen into disorder through inattention (like the *Xunzi*), he reorganized the textual field of early imperial China, thereby constituting several new intellectual disciplines. His son reworked Liu Xiang's preliminary catalogue into the *Seven Summaries* (*qi lüe* 七略) which was largely followed in Ban Gu's "Monograph on the Arts and Letters [*yi wen zhi* 藝文志]" in his *Book of the Han*.[112]

The Lius' project was based on the idea (as in the Renaissance and Reformation in early modern Europe) that one reached the truth by returning to the classical works themselves, abandoning the centuries of orally transmitted commentary that defined the teachings of court-appointed erudites. In this they participated in a broader movement in which scholars and writers – Yang Xiong, Huan Tan, Ban Gu, Wang Chong, and lesser authors – described the early sages from Fu Xi to Confucius as universal intellects and passionate authors. This was contrasted with the imperial erudites who focused on a single interpretation of a single text, thereby radically distorting the text itself and losing hope of achieving understanding.[113]

As part of this project of returning to the classic texts, Liu Xiang and Liu Xin collected and restored earlier texts on diagnosis and therapy, and in their bibliographic catalogue drew disparate therapies together under the rubric of *yi*. Although they still placed drug formulae, sexual arts, and techniques of

[112] On the early absence of an integrated field of "medicine," and the fundamental work of Liu Xiang in first defining such a field and giving it a history, see Brown, *The Art of Medicine in Early China*, ch. 4. This same point, and how a field of science-based medicine was defined, is discussed in Paul Unschuld, *Was ist Medizin: Westliche und östliche Wege der Heilkunst* (Munich: C. H. Beck, 2003), pp. 55–92. On the principles of Ban Gu's monograph and its structuring of the textual and intellectual world at the end of the Western Han, see Mark Edward Lewis, *Writing and Authority in Early China* (Albany: SUNY Press, 1999), pp. 325–332.

[113] Mark Edward Lewis, *Honor and Shame in Early China* (Cambridge: Cambridge University Press, 2021), pp. 187–205; Michael Nylan, *Yang Xiong and the Pleasures of Reading and Classical Learning in China* (New Haven: American Oriental Society, 2011), pp. 104–105, 113–115.

immortality into separate categories, these were then grouped as "methods and techniques" (*fang ji* 方技). They accompanied these with the earliest surviving list of exemplary healers, thus creating a proto-history of the new discipline of medicine.[114] This exemplifies the common pattern that when a discipline or mode of thought first emerges, people construct an imagined genealogy in which received names are recognized as early exemplars of the new practice. However, it is important to note that while Brown correctly posits this catalogue as a crucial step in constituting medicine as an intellectual and textual field, it is still a subset of a broader field of "methods and techniques" that protect, restore, and improve the body. It would take some centuries for the first two subcategories – medicine and formulae – to become a purely "medical" realm, while the sexual arts and techniques of immortality became aspects of religious Daoism.[115]

Before proceeding, we should note that this emergence of the categorized book collection, effectively a library although a tightly closed one, marks a set of major developments in the relation between men and texts. First, it shows that the amount of written material was too great to be mastered by any individual or single group. Second, it demonstrates the existence of an organization, here the imperial state and elements of the classicist scholars, who were committed to collecting and organizing the works of numerous previously isolated groups. Third, it is the product of a world where works are seen as traces of a vanished or vanishing era (in this case the era of the sages that ended with Confucius) that must be maintained through *scholarly* activity. Fourth, it marks an explicit claim of the overarching organization that sponsors the library to eliminate or absorb "esoteric" texts which had been the exclusive property of a self-selected group of masters formed through a process of mutual recognition and protracted training, a process that deliberately excluded the wider scholarly world. Finally, in the process of organizing the entirety of the texts that they could find, bibliographers (like the Lius) grouped previously disparate texts into new categories and disciplines, such as the overarching category of "methods and techniques" and sub-category of "medical classics," placing all these categories

[114] Ban Gu 班固, *Han shu* 漢書 (Beijing: Zhonghua, 1962), ch. 30, pp. 1776–1780. The *yi* classics are on p. 1776, the formulae texts on pp. 1777–1778, texts on sexual techniques on pp. 1778–1779, texts on immortality techniques on pp. 1779–1780, and the comprehensive rubric, which they glossed as an aspect of government, and list of healers on p. 1780. See Brown, *The Art of Medicine in Early China*, pp. 105–107.

[115] On the importance of "technical" fields as aspects of Han elite intellectual culture, see Michael Nylan and Mark Csikszentmihalyi, eds., *Technical Arts in the Han Histories: Tables and Treatises in the Shiji and Hanshu* (Albany: SUNY Press, 2021); Michael Nylan and Michael Loewe, eds., *China's Early Empires: A Re-appraisal* (Cambridge: Cambridge University Press, 2010), Part 3, "Technical Arts." On health and bodies see Vivienne Lo and Li Jianmin, "Manuscripts, Received Texts and Healing Arts," pp. 367–397.

into a comprehensive "knowledge tree" that would be visible to anyone who had sufficient time and resources to achieve the necessary literacy.[116]

As an example of the creation of such new disciplines within a knowledge tree, the Lius categorization of medicine is significant. Most important, the category under which it was grouped was explicitly defined as "methods and techniques." The catalogue of the Lius and Ban Gu carried forward the tensions that we observed in the story of the Attendant He and Zichan, and in the polemics of Chunyu Yuyi against named physicians or an anonymous crowd of healers whose arts could not match his own text-based diagnoses and formulae. These stories pitted a more generalized intellect tied into the political and philosophical order against the limited specialization of someone who was a master of only one art. In the same way, the Lius hierarchized their textual universe, placing on top the encompassing mental skills embodied in the classics and the philosophers (whose texts were arranged by the Lius themselves), to be followed by the inferior mental specializations of the military treatises, calendrics and astronomy, and finally the "methods and techniques" of perfecting the body (with each field assigned to a specialized official, although the Lius doubtless participated).[117]

However, while a discipline of technical medicine emerged in the re-working of the textual realm, at this point there were no texts with named authors or attributions to any recent author. Thus the most prestigious category, that of the "medical classics" (*yi jing* 醫經), consisted only of the *Yellow Emperor's Inner Classic* and *Outer Classic*, *Bian Que's Inner Classic* and *Outer Classic* (attributed to the mythic early physician whose "biography" precedes that of Chunyu Yi in the *Shi ji*), *Mr. Bai's Inner Classic* and *Outer Classic*, and the cryptic *Assisting Chapters* (*pang pian* 旁篇). The texts in the other categories have names that indicate their contents or attributions to such ancient, mythic figures as the Yellow Emperor, Shen Nong, and Bian Que. Despite the new prestige that such texts gained in the Lius classification, they remained collective works by anonymous authors. Not until the late Eastern Han and the century immediately after the Han did medical books appear with named authors who appended "postfaces" (*xu* 序) to explain and justify the work.[118]

116 Lewis, *Writing and Authority*, pp. 325–327. On libraries and their knowledge trees, see Alvin Kernan, *Printing Technology, Letters, and Samuel Johnson* (Princeton: Princeton University Press, 1987), pp. 245–246. On libraries in early China, see Jean-Pierre Drège, *Les bibliotheques en Chine au temps des manuscrits* (Paris: École Française d'Extrême-Orient, 1991). For a history of libraries, see Andrew Pettegree and Arthur der Werduwen, *The Library: A Fragile History* (New York: Basic Books, 2021).

117 Lewis, *Writing and Authority*, pp. 331–332.

118 Brown, *The Art of Medicine in Early China*, pp. 91, 96–98. This reflects the fact that only in the first and second centuries CE did writing become sufficiently prestigious that people celebrated devoting one's life to it. See Lewis, *Honor and Shame*, pp. 187–205. This in turn reflects a systematic re-working of the "literary field" of Eastern Han China, where different genres and

Consequently, the one surviving work which may provide insights into the development from the first century BCE to the late Eastern Han of ideas about body models, diagnosis, and therapy (focusing on acupuncture) is the *Huangdi neijing*. This title appears in the Han imperial catalogue under the *yi jing* rubric, although it is preserved only in its medieval recensions: the *Suwen* 素問, the *Lingshu* 靈樞, and the *Taisu* 太素.[119] As discussed by Unschuld, it seems that these works began to be assembled in the late Western Han and continued to develop through numerous hands over a long time. As the works drew together diverse texts and ideas, passed through multiple hands, and were doubtless jumbled and then reassembled in the centuries between the Eastern Han and the Tang, they are sometimes self-contradictory. A more systematic work on the uses of yin/yang and the Five Phases to articulate a medicine of systematic correspondences was compiled in the first or second century CE to reduce the confusion. This work, entitled the *Classic of Difficult Issues* [*nanjing* 難經], thus provides a more rigorous formulation of medical theory and practice in the Eastern Han, but the loss of the contradictions and tensions from the other recensions reduces the insights that it offers into the full range of medicine in the period.[120]

Thus, the *Suwen* and *Lingshu* compiled diverse texts and fragments written between the second century BCE and the second century CE, some perhaps

categories of texts were produced by diverse types of authors who earned their livings in distinct manners, and who selected the field in which they wrote through espousing the values defined by such texts. This process can be compared with the transformation of the literary field in nineteenth-century France, as analyzed in Pierre Bourdieu, *Les règles de l'art: Genèse et structure du champ littéraire* (Paris: Seuil, 1992).

119 Since the *Taisu* was compiled in the seventh century based on the *Suwen* and *Lingshu*, I will follow the conventional practice of using these latter two recensions. I cite Zhang Zhicong 張志聰, eds., *Huangdi neijing suwen jizhu* 黃帝內經素問集註, in *Zhongguo yixue dacheng* 中國醫學大成 (Shanghai: Shanghai Kexue Jishu Chubanshe, 1990); Zhang Zhicong, eds., *Huangdi neijing lingshu jizhu* 靈樞集註, in *Zhongguo yixue dacheng*. For English translations, see Paul Unschuld and Hermann Tessenow, in collaboration with Zhang Jinsheng, *Huang Di Nei Jing Su Wen: An Annotated Translation of Huang Di's Inner Classic – Basic Questions*, 2. Vols. (Berkeley: University of California Press, 2011); Unschuld, *Huang Di Nei Jing Ling Shu: The Ancient Chinese Classic on Needle Therapy, the Complete Chinese Text with an Annotated English Translation* (Berkeley: University of California Press, 2016). For the *Taisu*, see *Huangdi neijing taisu* 太素, compiled by Yang Shangshan 楊上善 (Sui dynasty) (Beijing: Renmin Weisheng Chubanshe, 1965). See also Cai Biming 蔡壁名, *Shenti yu ziran: yi "Huangdi ne jing suwen" wei zhongxin lun gudai sixiang zhong de shenti guan* 身體與自然:以"皇帝內經素文"為中心論古代思想中的身體觀 (Taipei: Taiwan Daxue Chubanshe, 1997).

120 On dating the *Suwen* and *Lingshu*, see Unschuld, *Huang Di Nei Jing Su Wen*, pp. 1–7. On the compilation of the text, see also David Joseph Keegan, "The 'Huang-ti Nei-ching': The Structure of the Compilation; The Significance of the Structure," Ph. D. dissertation, University of California at Berkeley, 1988. Unschuld has also translated the *Nanjing*, including commentaries from later centuries. See *Nan-ching: The Classic of Difficult Issues*, translated and annotated by Paul Unschuld (Berkeley: University of California Press, 1986). The "Prolegomena," pp. 1–59, discusses its dating and contents. For the importance to the

related to recently excavated texts, with some additions being made in the subsequent centuries. This process depended upon the simultaneous emergence of a "community of literati and literary patrons who collected, disseminated, and made use of the texts," as exemplified in the bibliographic treatise of the *Book of the Han*. This treatise also notably omits many of the titles that have been recently excavated, demonstrating that it aimed at being comprehensive only in the sense of collecting all texts *approved* by the classicizing literati acting as agents of the state order.[121] In this way the simultaneous processes of textualization, systematization, synthesis, and dissemination underlay the creation of medicine as a technical discipline articulated in freely circulating (within the extreme physical limits of the period) texts by those expert in their interpretation and employment. This circulation of texts became fundamental to the new type of healer who was emerging, just as in Reformation Germany municipal physicians devoted themselves to book collecting and anatomical experimentation even as they battled to replace apothecaries as the model practitioners of medicine.[122]

One interesting feature of the Yellow Emperor corpus is that it either set the model for or adopted the Lius' categorization of the emergent field of medicine as a "technique" or an "art." Both the *Suwen* and the *Lingshu* describe what their healers do as a *shu* 術, which was largely synonymous with the term *ji* used in the imperial catalogue for the arts of healing or improving the embodied self.[123] They also describe healers as "craftsmen" (*gong* 工), assimilating their art to those of other skillful practitioners who provided for people's needs.[124] While the term seemingly indicates a lower social status, resembling that of a manual worker, the authors were also using the adjectival sense of *gong* as "skillful" or

emergence of acupuncture of the cosmological and numerological theories expounded in the *Nanjing*, see Li Jianmin 李建民, *Si sheng zhi yu: Zhou Qin Han maixue zhi yuanliu* 私生之域: 周秦漢脈學之源流 (Taipei: Zhongyang Yanjiuyuan Lishi Yuyan Yanjiusuo, 2000).

121 Unschuld, *Huang Di Nei Jing Su Wen*, pp. 76–77. On the library as a social institution devoted to preserving a canonical order, see Kernan, *Printing Technology*, ch. 1, 4, 5, 7–8; Kernan, *The Imaginary Library: An Essay on Literature and Society* (Princeton: Princeton University Press, 1982).

122 Hannah Murphy, *A New Order of Medicine: The Rise of Physicians in Reformation Nuremberg* (Pittsburgh: University of Pittsburgh Press, 2019). For a similar process in later times, see Lester S. King, *The Philosophy of Medicine: The Early Eighteenth Century* (Cambridge, Mass.: Harvard University Press, 1978).

123 *Suwen jizhu*, ch. 5:40, p. 46; ch. 9:77, pp. 11, 12; ch. 7:83, p. 50; *Lingshu jizhu*, ch. 1:1, p. 14.

124 *Suwen jizhu*, ch. 2:9, pp. 30, 31; ch. 2:13, p. 15; ch. 2:14, pp. 17 (2), 18; ch. 4:25, p. 30 (this refers to the throng of mediocre doctors as *zhong gong*, just as Chunyu Yi called them *zhong yi*); ch. 4:26, pp. 33, 34–35 (6); ch. 4:27, p. 40; ch. 5:35, pp. 25, 26; ch. 6:54, p. 11; ch. 8:74, pp. 2, 29, 33 (this presents the hierarchy of physicians based on levels of skill); ch. 9:76, pp. 5, 7; ch. 9:77, pp. 9–12 (6); ch. 9:78, p. 13; ch. 9:81, p. 26; *Lingshu jizhu*, ch. 1:4, p. 40 (5); ch. 1:5, p. 64 (4); ch. 1:7, p. 79; ch, 4:35, p. 33; ch. 6: 49, p. 41; ch. 7:55, p. 2 (3); ch. 7:59, p. 19; ch. 7:60, p. 31; ch. 9:73, pp. 12, 15–16, 16 (2), 17; ch. 9:79, p. 78.

"expert," as indicated in a passage where the use of *gong* to indicate a healer is the lowest of a hierarchical series rising from the ordinary practitioner to the "skillful" (*qiao* 巧), the "spirit-like" (*shen*), and ultimately the "sage" (*sheng*). Moreover, elsewhere *gong* is placed above the "crude" or "incompetent" (*cu* 粗).[125] In other lists the skillful *gong* still figures below the "enlightened" (*ming*) and the "spirit-like" (*shen*).[126] These comparative hierarchies show that the new-style physicians placed themselves among the elite intellects.

Describing the highest form of healer as a sage, which recurs throughout the texts, also draws them into the realm of philosophers and rulers, thus reinforcing the elevation of status indicated by constituting healing as a textual category. This claim to sagehood also maps onto, and indeed justifies, the use of the early imperial state as a central metaphor for the human body, with the organs that stored the different forms of energetic substances being identified as "palaces" and "depots," and the overarching structure of the body with its vessels along which energies moved following the way material resources of the empire moved along the river systems and roads.[127]

This emergence of a practice of medicine based on the circulation of theoretical and technical texts entailed the gradual suppression (without elimination, as all earlier practices continued) of the range of healers who had thrived in the early Han. It shifted away from multiple patient-centered, curative traditions to a scientifically grounded, technical practice which privileged the theoretical knowledge of the physician, basing itself on models of the cosmos and numerology to claim superiority over the limited practices of earlier healers. Even more significantly, these new-style healers, who were the model "persons" created in the new texts, asserted their authority over the people who had previously developed and healed their own bodies, but were now reduced to the level of a patient whose body could be understood and healed only by the physician.

Indeed, the first chapter of the *Suwen* in its present form insists on the need to abandon the diverse earlier regimes of nourishing and perfecting the self

125 *Suwen jizhu*, ch. 8:74, p. 33. On the ordinary practitioner as superior to the "crude," see, for example, *Lingshu jizhu*, ch. 1:1, pp. 2, 3; ch. 1:3, p. 2 (2); ch. 1:9, p. 103; ch. 2:11, p. 66; ch. 5:44, p. 40; ch. 6:48, p. 24 (here *gong* is an inferior version of a "teacher of the whole world" [*tianxia shi* 天下師]). Sometimes the crude are also contrasted with the "outstanding" (*shang* 上), and *gong* are rated as outstanding, middle, or lower.

126 *Lingshu jizhu*, ch. 1:4, p. 39 (2).

127 Unschuld, *Medicine in China: A History of Ideas*, pp. 77–83; *Huang Di Nei Jing Su Wen*, pp. 36–38, 133–136, 288–289, 340–342, 435; *Huang Di Nei Jing Ling Shu*, pp. 11–12. For examples of the political metaphor, or image of the body as a microcosm, scattered through the Yellow Emperor corpus see *Suwen jizhu*, ch. 1:2, p. 11; ch. 1:3, pp. 11, 19; ch. 2a:5, p. 13; ch. 2:8, p. 26; ch. 2a:9, p. 27; ch. 2a:12, pp. 10–12; ch. 3:21, p. 11; ch. 4:27, p. 40; *Lingshu jizhu*, ch. 1:1, pp. 1–2; ch. 2:12, p. 73; ch. 4:29, p. 13; ch. 4:35, pp. 32–33; ch. 5:37, pp. 1–2; ch. 6:49, p. 32; ch. 9:81, pp. 89–90. See also Yates, "Body, Space, Time and Bureaucracy."

through the hygienic practices of exercise, sex, and diet, arguing through quotations from earlier historians and philosophers.[128] The Yellow Emperor, after following a magical path to adulthood (largely copied from the *Shi ji*'s account), asks Qi Bo why people in antiquity had lived more than one hundred years while remaining mobile, vigorous, and strong, while people of the present day are already disintegrating by the age of fifty. Qi Bo replies, in a passage borrowing phrases and ideas from the *Huainanzi*, that people in antiquity patterned their actions on the cycles of yin and yang, ate and drank in moderation, were regular in sleeping, and eschewed pointless activities, so their bodies (*xing* 形) and spirits (*shen*) remained joined. In contrast to these ideal beings in the distant past, the people of the present day regularly drink wine, behave badly, have sex while drunk, (echoing cases of Chunyu Yi) and thereby exhaust their body's energies.[129]

Qi Bo then describes the sages of high antiquity who taught their people how to avoid harmful winds, abide in quiet, conserve their *qi*, have few desires, and eschew strong feelings. The people enjoyed their simple food and clothing, avoided all disturbing emotions, and did not envy those of higher status. After a lengthy, numerologically structured account of human maturation and decline, Qi Bo explains how those who have the Way can "repel old age" (*que lao* 却老), preserve their physical form, and still produce children at the age of one hundred. The chapter concludes with the Yellow Emperor describing how in high antiquity the "true people" (*zhen ren*) through imitating yin and yang and proper breathing could preserve their spirit and keep muscles and flesh united. This is followed by a sequence of decline adapted from the *Zhuangzi* from the "perfected people" (*zhi ren*) through the sages, and finally the worthy, who were able to live in harmony with the seasons, accumulate essential energies, still cravings and emotions, and thus to live out shorter life spans which still reaching one hundred. This chapter thus begins the book with an account of earlier times when people extended their lives by imitating nature and practicing

---

128 *Suwen jizhu*, ch. 1, pp. 1–7; Unschuld and Tessenow, *Su Wen*, pp. 29–44. This model of an ideal antiquity when people achieved perfect health, in this case through mastery of emotions, in contrast with the degenerate people of the present age, is also discussed in *Suwen jizhu*, ch. 2:13, p. 13; Unschuld and Tessenow, *Su Wen*, pp. 220–222. A historical model of decline in the use of medicinal decoctions is in *Suwen jizhu*, ch. 2:14, pp. 16–17; Unschuld and Tessenow, *Su Wen*, pp. 234–237.

129 *Shi ji*, ch. 1, p. 1; *Huainanzi*, ch. 2, pp. 20–21, 22–23. This emphasis on the *shen* at the beginning of the *Suwen* is developed in the *Lingshu*, whose eighth chapter entitled "Rooted in the Spirits" (*ben shen* 本神) explores how personal health and well-being depend on guiding *shen* through the passages of the *mai* into the heart. See *Lingshu jizhu*, ch. 1:8, pp. 80–86; Unschuld, *Ling Shu*, pp. 147–153; Claude Larre and Elisabeth Rochat de la Vallée, *Rooted in Spirit: The Heart of Chinese Medicine*, tr. Sarah Stang (Barrytown: Station Hill Press, 1995). This last is a translation with extensive commentary of the text, focusing on the passions as the fundamental manifestation of *qi* within the person, and the key to all forms of therapy.

hygienic therapies, but radically opposing this to the present day when the ability to keep body and spirit intact by self-mastery and exercise had been lost through a long process of decline.

Over its vast expanse, and without achieving consistency, the *Huangdi neijing* elaborates versions of the categories used by Harper to analyze the Mawangdui materials: a model of the body, a theory of disease, and types of therapy. As for the first, its model of the body developed a more systematic version of earlier vessel texts, moving from an idea of the vessels as unlinked channels where *qi* connected upper parts to lower ones, to a vision of a single connected system where *qi* circulated throughout the body. In its general omission of alternative therapies and modes of self-cultivation, it also posited a body where the moving *qi* was the single, crucial element and the channels the decisive constituents of the person. While the texts do not define what *qi* is, they agree that it is airy, light, constantly in motion, and essential for maintaining life. As discussed in the sections on theories of the person elaborated by the philosophers, this emphasis on the body as consisting of, or a container for, *qi* (and its more refined forms as "essence" [*jing*] and "spirit" [*shen*)) patterned the self on a social model in which the more refined and mobile elements corresponded to the elites who wielded their minds, as opposed to the coarser, physical limbs and muscles that matched the laboring masses.[130] In the context of medicine, knowing the body as *qi* entailed a set of propositions about the patient *as a person*, about his relation to the doctor, and about the capacities of the doctor to know him or her.

The relations of the types of *qi* and the person took several forms. First, as Unschuld elaborates, the organs of the human body are defined as "depots" or "containers" of more dynamic substances, and ranked hierarchically according to the substance that they contain. This locating of substances also leads to observations on the links between inner organs and the exterior, secondary parts of the body, for example, skin, sinews, flesh, and bone. While the individual chapters do not agree on all these questions, and sometimes even contradict themselves, the hierarchical sequencing of moving substances, storage depots, and exterior parts remains consistent. This pattern maps the body onto the state, thus developing ideas about health within the context of establishing a political order, and facilitates the claims of those for whom the practice of medicine was identified with participating in the textual universe established through the state.[131]

130 This theory goes even further in the *Nanjing*, which replaces references to *mai* with the term *jing* 經, which in its senses of "guiding principle," "universality," and consequently "canonical text" insists on both the cosmic and political images of the body. See Unschuld, *Nan-ching*, *passim*; Linck, "Der poetische Körper von Mawangdui," p. 16; Lewis, *Writing and Authority*, pp. 297–300.

131 Unschuld, *Huang Di Nei Jing Su Wen*, pp. 127–144.

The model of a body as structured through the movement and storage of *qi* also facilitated linking medical ideas to the theories of yin and yang and the Five Phases, which had become fundamental to theorizing different realms by mapping them onto each other through numerology. Perhaps even more important, the definition of the body through *qi* facilitated articulating ideas about the links between the individual person and the cosmos. Thus chapter 3 of the *Suwen* is entitled "Discourse on How the *Qi* of Life Penetrates to Heaven [*sheng qi tong tian lun* 生氣通天論]" and elaborates a theory in which the body had to fuse its energies with those of Heaven and Earth through following the time of day, time of year, and point in history. Such fusion also hinged on correctly employing various factors structured according to yin and yang, or grouped into sets of five, for example, emotions, flavors, and seasons, to guide the body and its conduct.[132] This blurring of the boundaries between the self and the cosmos was an enduring feature of the *qi* discourse, as discussed in the first section.

A third significant feature of defining the body through its *qi* (and the more refined substances) was to facilitate understanding self and body through emphasizing the role of emotions. As early as passages attributed to Confucius, blood and *qi* were regarded as driving energies which manifested themselves in emotions and passions, *qi* being conflated with human violence and bellicosity. Moreover, late Warring States philosophers devoted considerable attention to a self-mastery that focused on control of emotions.[133] As Shigehisa Kuriyama has discussed, in Eastern Han medical literature the reading of *qi* in the vessels was conflated with these ideas, so that increasingly the art of reading pulses became not just a means of diagnosing diseases, but also a way to recognize a person's character. Thus, the physical state of the body and the nature of the person's character fused both in the observation of emotions, the dynamic interface between what we would view as body and mind, and in the pulses which were the fluid manifestation of these energies. Emotions also provided a meeting ground between what the new-style physicians observed in their patients and what they perceived in themselves. As Kuriyama argues, "The deepest certainties about *qi* were rooted in knowledge that people had of the body because they *were*, themselves bodies." This *qi* which defined the self was both external, in the perceptions of pulses and the face's color, and internal in the physician's perceptions of his own experiences.[134]

132 *Suwen jizhu*, pp. 11–19; Unschuld and Tessenow, *Su Wen*, pp. 59–81. Some of the same points repeat in ch. 4, and "penetrating to Heaven" or "to the Heavenly *qi*" as the basis of life is also discussed in ch. 2:9, p. 28; Unschuld and Tessenow, *Su Wen*, p. 167.

133 Lewis, *Sanctioned Violence*, ch. 6. The passages from Confucius are cited on p. 222.

134 Kuriyama, "Part One, Styles of Touching," *The Expressiveness of the Body*, especially pp. 102–104. On emotions in the Neijing, see also Wolfgang Schulz, *Die Auffassung der Emotionen im Huang Di Nei Jing und ihre Brechung in der Affektlogik Luc Ciompis* (Berlin: Europäischer

While the early philosophers had primarily viewed emotions as a destructive force that drained the body's energies or trapped the mind in improper responses, most references to emotions in the Yellow Emperor corpus treat them as symptoms of internal conditions. A preponderance of these treat feelings as conditions that the doctor must observe to deduce problems with the *qi*, whether blockages, reversals, or other failings. They are also cited, though less frequently, to allow the physician to judge the progress of a therapy. Finally, sometimes the physician uses the emotional condition of his patient to decide that certain therapies are too dangerous. In some cases, emotions are also more traditionally cited as the cause of ailments, but these are not frequent. In short, the internal state of the patient has become primarily an objective condition which the doctor observes to guide his diagnoses and therapy, rather than something subjective that the patient himself observes and seeks to master through the powers of an intellect developed in hygienic exercises.

This approach to the emotions also helps explain another innovation in the Yellow Emperor corpus. Earlier texts had discussed the hierarchy of organs in the body, and the division of labor between them, often employing the metaphor of the state with the heart/mind assigned the role of ruler. Such earlier metaphors focused on the dangers posed by the senses which figured in the role of ministers that had to be mastered by the ruler/mind, although the *Mencius* also used the idea of the mind as ruler to justify the political dominance of "those who toiled with their minds" over those who used physical strength. In the Yellow Emperor corpus, however, even in a rare case where the mind was described as ruler, this was due to its being the storehouse of the highest substances, and most lists of organs do not place them in a hierarchy.[135]

Universitätsverlag, 2009); Luc Ciompi, *Die emotionalen Grundlagen des Denkens: Entwurf einer fraktalen Affektlogik* (Göttingen: Vandenhoeck & Ruprecht, 1997). The most comprehensive discussion of emotions, which directly follows the Yellow Emperor's question of how diseases are caused by *qi*, is in *Suwen*, ch. 5:39, pp. 44–45; Unschuld and Tessenow, *Su Wen*, pp. 593–597. For other discussions scattered through the corpus, see *Suwen jizhu*, ch. 1:1, pp. 2 (2), 3 (2), 6 (2); ch. 1:2, p. 7; ch. 1:3, pp. 12, 13–14; ch. 2a:5, pp. 5, 7, 8–9, 10, 11; ch. 2a:8, p. 25; ch. 2a:9, pp. 32–33; ch. 2b:10, pp. 2, 6 (2); ch. 2b:13, pp. 13, 16; ch. 2b:14, p. 17; ch. 3:16, pp. 5–6, 8; ch. 3:17, pp. 9–10 (2), 13; ch. 3:19, pp. 35, 37; ch. 4:21, pp. 10–11; ch. 4:22, p. 19; ch. 4:23, pp. 22 (2), 24; ch. 4:24, pp. 25–27; ch. 4:25, p. 31; ch. 4:30, pp. 53–54; ch. 5:32, pp. 6–7; ch. 5:35, p. 27; ch. 5:36, pp. 29–31, 34; ch. 5:40, p. 47; ch. 5:42, pp. 59–60 (4); ch. 5:43, pp. 62, 63; ch. 5:44, p. 68; ch. 5:45, pp. 74–75; ch. 5:46, pp. 77–78; ch. 5:47, p. 84; ch. 5:48, pp. 85 (3), 88, 90; ch. 5:49, pp. 93–96 (5); ch. 6:50, p. 2; ch. 6:52, p. 6; ch. 7:60, p. 19 (2); ch. 7:62, pp. 31, 33, 35 (3), 36–37 (3); ch. 7:63, pp. 45, 47; ch. 7:64, pp. 51, 53 (2); ch. 8:67, pp. 14, 15 (3), 16; ch. 8:69, pp. 37, 38, 41, 48; ch. 8:70, pp. 51(2), 52 (2), 57, 64; ch. 8c:74, pp. 6, 9 (4), 10, 12, 13, 15, 16 (3), 31, 34, 36, 37; ch. 9:75, p. 3; ch. 9:76, pp. 4, 5, 6 (2); ch. 9:77, pp. 9, 10, 11, 12; ch. 9:79, p. 18; ch. 9:80, pp. 22, 23, 25; ch. 9:81, pp. 26 (2), 27 (3).

[135] This, and other aspects of ideas about a composite body, are discussed in Lewis, *The Construction of Space*, pp. 36–61. The passages in the *Neijing* are discussed on pp. 38–39, 324–325, note #96. See also Raphals, *Tripartite Self*, ch. 6.

The most plausible explanation for this break with earlier practice is that the earlier metaphor of brain as ruler emerged from a model of an active intellect working to master its own self, both its mental and physical aspects, while the emergent model in the *Neijing* focused on the mind of the physician, reducing the patient to an object of therapy. This hypothesis is supported by the fact that while the texts refer to the mind of the patient only where its disorders shape diagnosis and therapy, they insist on the need for the physician to be focused and calm. Some passages even describe the healer observing and guiding the patient's "will and thoughts" (*zhi yi* 志意), applying his "spirit illumination" (*shen ming*) to the person of the patient, or focusing and applying his "essential spirit" (*jing shen*) to the process of needling to restore order to the patient's mind. One of the most striking accounts of the physician's mental mastery taking charge of the patient is the advocacy of seeking "oneness" or "union" that is declared to be the highest form of healing and described as follows:

> Close the door and shut the windows. Bind yourself to the patient, repeatedly inquiring about his feelings, in order that you can adapt yourself to his thoughts (*yi*). If you get hold of his spirit (*shen*) the patient will flourish, but if you lose it he will perish.[136]

Having sealed themselves together in a dark room, the physician is urged to mentally unite with the patient to fully restore his "spirits," which are the highest energetic or mental substance in accounts of the embodied self. This emphasis on the refined forms of *qi* as the medium through which the healer and the patient come together, and through which the former shapes the latter, are an extension of the idea discussed above in the "Introduction" that *qi* facilitates theorizing the convergence of people (as distinct foci) into a broader "field" or "atmosphere" where all of them achieve fuller personhood through membership in the group.[137]

---

136 *Suwen jizhu*, ch.2b:11, p. 9; ch. 2b:13, pp. 15–16 (this describes achieving "oneness" with the patient); ch. 2b:14, p. 17 (total spirit focused into needling); ch. 3:16, pp. 5, 7; ch. 4:25, pp. 29, 29–30, 31; ch. 4:26, p. 36 (when the physician's focused mind advances, he alone can perceive and understand the nature of the disease); ch. 4:27, pp. 38–39; ch. 6:54, p. 11 (after describing the physician's concentration while needling, it concludes that he must look the patient in the eye and "control his spirit" (*zhi qi shen* 制其神), so that the *qi* will flow easily); ch. 7:58, p. 6; ch. 7:62, p. 39; ch. 9:78, p. 13; ch. 9:80, p. 25; *Lingshu jizhu*, ch. 1:1, pp. 2–3; ch. 6:49, p. 41; ch. 1:9, pp. 102–103; ch. 5:42, pp. 26–27; ch. 5:45, p. 44; ch. 6:48, p. 24; ch. 6:52, pp. 53–55; ch. 7:60, pp. 27–28; ch. 9:73, p. 17; ch. 9:78, p. 63. For examples of this argument that describe the ideal healer as a sage, see *Suwen jizhu*, ch. 1:3, pp. 12, 16–17; ch. 2b:5, p. 6; ch. 2b:12, p. 12; ch. 2b:13, pp. 14, 15; ch. 8a:66, pp. 1–2 (here the sage is defined by his using spirit with no prescribed method); ch. 9:73, pp. 9–10; ch. 9:77, p. 9; ch. 9:80, p. 24.

137 These ideas are also discussed by a contemporary Japanese scholar studying early Chinese theories of *qi* as a background to ideas that developed later in Buddhism and in Japanese society (as well as providing comparisons with certain modern European thinkers). See Ichiro Yamaguchi, *Ki als leibhaftige Vernunft: Beitrag zur interkulturellen Phänomenologie*

This shift of focus from the embodied self to a therapist who guides a person as a patient also figures in one passage which transfers the hygienic self-cultivation practices advocated in the "nourishing life" tradition entirely to the person of the physician. This describes how there are five principles to proper needling of which ordinary people are all ignorant. These five are ordering the spirit (*zhi shen* 治神), nourishing the body, judging the reliability of drugs, preparing pointed stones, and mastering the diagnosis of blood and *qi*. This reiterates the program of the Mawangdui corpus, except that here it is entirely deployed as a preliminary to the doctor's attaining the total self-mastery and concentration that enable him to properly needle the patient.[138]

As for the theories of disease in the Yellow Emperor corpus, they basically carry forward the categories of the earlier vessel texts, shifting emphasis to the "functional" or "physiological," where disease is understood not as an invader but as a disturbance in the functioning of the body itself, in this case largely in the flow of *qi*. While ontological theories of disease as an invader still exist, the "invaders" are almost never "bugs" or "demons," but instead environmental factors such as "wind" (the most common external source of disease), but also damp, cold, heat, or dryness. These new models of disease highlight the impact of focusing on *qi* as the primary substance in the body. The physiological diseases are attributed to poor lifestyle (as in many of Chunyu Yi's cases), to actions undertaken at the inappropriate season, or to mental problems that induce bodily distress. Thus, while patients no longer play a major role in healing or improving their bodies, they often figure as a way of explaining the disease's origins.[139]

Theories of treatment in the Yellow Emperor corpus, like theories of disease, largely inherited the ideas of the vessel literature found at Mawangdui and Zhangjiashan. Diagnosis was primarily based on taking pulses, still supplemented by examining the patient's complexion. Therapy was dominated by acupuncture, and in the *Lingshu* discussions of needling supplanted all the other forms of therapy. The *Suwen* still occasionally discussed other forms, including bloodletting, using drugs, and applying heat.[140] However, the move toward a model of the body based almost entirely on *qi* and its derivatives entailed the predominance of diagnoses and therapies that explicitly targeted such substances. Moreover, emphasizing the self-cultivation and mental mastery of the

---

der Leiblichkeit (Munich: Wilhelm Fink Verlag, 1997), ch. 2 "Das Ki als Fundament der Zwischen-leiblichkeit" and ch. 4.

138 *Suwen jizhu*, ch. 4:25, pp. 29–31.

139 Unschuld, *Huang Di Nei Jing Su Wen*, ch. 7–8; Unschuld, *Huang Di Nei Jing Ling Shu*, ch. 15–25. On wind as a major factor, see Kuriyama, *The Expressiveness of the Body*, ch. 6.

140 Unschuld, *Huang Di Nei Jing Su Wen*, ch. 9–12.

healer also led to focusing on his abilities to read pulses, discern the hidden messages of complexions, and to place and time the movement of the needles to properly guide the *qi* of his patient.

This emphasis on diagnosis through the pulses and complexion, and on therapy through acupuncture (and to a lesser degree moxibustion) explains how the interfaces between the core of the body and the outer environment became the privileged zones for any understanding and modification of the self. *Qi* as the dynamic and determinative element in the body, and wind as the exterior substance that provided the medium for environmental influences and any external origins of disease, moved in and out through the porous boundaries of the skin, and the system of acupuncture meridians entailed that what Western medicine defines as "internal" organs were manipulable at the body's surface. Both the earlier accounts that were incorporated into the new genealogy of medicine, and the Yellow Emperor corpus itself, described diseases that moved from the outside inward, growing more difficult to cure as they penetrated more deeply. Thus, the mastery of the physician, and his ability to help the patient, depended on recognizing the disease at its earliest stage, that is, at the level of the skin.[141]

This aspect of the new theory of medicine thus emphasized the ability of the doctor to recognize the onset of diseases before they had become visible to lesser people, including the patient, and to predict the course of their development. The clearest articulation of this idea was not in the Yellow Emperor corpus, but in the writings of Hua Tuo (141–208 CE), who followed a discussion of the relation of pulses with *qi*, by stating, "The pulse is the first sign/presage of *qi* and blood."[142] This assimilated the insistence on the importance of early recognition to the broader idea, which figured in numerous fields from military texts to yarrow divination, that anyone who could recognize a trend at its beginning could easily master it, while delay that allowed it to achieve full form would make it impossible to handle. In this way the art of the

[141] Lewis, *The Construction of Space*, pp. 61–63, pp. 337–338 notes #209–217. The major early story on this theme was the account in the *Han Feizi* of the visits of Bian Que to Lord Huan of Qi. At the first visit he recognized the disease at the skin and could have dealt with it, but neither the lord nor his courtiers saw any disease and declined to do anything. At each later visit the disease went deeper but was still ignored, until it reached the bone marrow and became impossible to cure. See *Han Feizi xin jiao zhu*, ch. 7:21 "Yu Lao," p. 441; *Shi ji*, ch. 105, p. 2793. On the progressive penetration of wind-introduced diseases from the pores to the marrow (or internal organs), see *Suwen jizhu*, ch. 1:2, pp. 10–11 (here the sage only treats incipient diseases); ch. 2:14, p. 17; ch. 4:26, p. 35; ch. 5:35, p. 26; ch. 6:50, pp. 1–2; ch. 7:62, pp. 36–37; ch. 7:63, p. 41; *Lingshu jizhu*, ch. 7:60, pp. 27–28; ch. 9:73, p. 16.

[142] Hua Tuo 華佗, *Zhongzang jing* 中藏經 (Beijing: Airusheng Shuzihua Jishu Yanjiu Zhongxin, 2009), ch. 10, p. 1; translated as *Master Hua's Classic of the Central Viscera: A Translation of Hua Tuo's Zhong Zang Jing* (Boulder: Blue Poppy Press, 1993), ch. 10, p. 29.

physician was again adapted to that of the philosopher or man of state (and as Miranda Brown has argued, the story of Bian Que and Lord Huan cast the "healer" in the role of the political adviser).

One final impact of the emergence of the model of the human body in vessel theory was that it was ungendered, so that most modern scholars date the emergence of any medical theorization of women's bodies to the Tang and the Song. However, Robin Yates has shown that medicine for women can be dated back to the Han and the pre-Han, and in a recent article Li Yunxin has demonstrated that the healing traditions that preceded the Yellow Emperor corpus discussed women in numerous contexts.[143] To summarize her article, the early texts on nourishing life and certain modes of healing discuss gendered patients, gendered medicines, gendered diseases (as the embodiment of yin and yang), gendered sexual partners, the female as mother, and gendered healers. In the technical medicine defined by the Yellow Emperor corpus, these distinctions tend to disappear. Li Yunxin hypothesizes that, within the limits of currently available texts, the emergent technical medicine largely suppressed many of these themes as part of its efforts to claim hegemony in the field of healing. Although the earlier methods of healing and self-cultivation were still practiced, they were dominated by the new science-based, textual medical field established in the Eastern Han. She also cites Robin Yates's remarks on Zhang Ji's detailed discussions in the *Jin gui yao lüe* of the mother's medical problems that arise during pregnancy, speculating that this was associated with the rising attention to the mother as the center of the family in the Eastern Han elite.[144]

This reference to the Eastern Han elite also points back to the theme of ritual which, in the form of funerary rites, was crucial to self-definition among this group. Specifically, as discussed by K. E. Brashier, the stereotyped postmortem remembrance of these families' dead was a process of pouring the newly deceased into prefabricated molds through which they became ancestors. Their posthumous names were chosen from a limited and predetermined pool, their social identity was fixed through asserting their kinship relations to the living, they were described with set phrases from classical literature, and their identities were set as resembling a given cultural hero or sage official from antiquity.[145] This system of turning individual persons into creatures defined

[143] Robin D. S. Yates, "Medicine for Women in Early China: A Preliminary Survey," *NAN NÜ* 7.2 (October 2005): 127–181; Li Yunxin, "Representations of Gender in Early Chinese Medicine: A Prehistory of *Fuke*," *Bulletin of the Jao Tsung-I Academy of Sinology*, Issue 9 (2022).

[144] Miranda Brown, *The Politics of Mourning in Early China* (Albany: SUNY Press, 2007); Mark Edward Lewis, "Mothers and Sons in Early Imperial China," *Extrême Orient, Extrême Occident*, Hors-série 2012, pp. 245–276.

[145] K. E. Brashier, *Public Memory in Early China* (Cambridge, Mass.: Harvard University Press, 2014).

entirely by genealogical relations to the living (who in turn were bound to each other through their shared relation to the dead), and their participation in standardized social roles and virtues, marked the culmination in the late Han of classical mourning ritual as a means of creating selves within the networks of their kinship groups.

A final important late Eastern Han development in ideas about the embodied self was the appearance of the first technical medical texts identified as the work of named authors, specifically Hua Tuo and Zhang Ji. Particularly important were the works of Zhang Ji (ca. 150–219 CE), which currently survive as the *Shang han lun* [傷寒論 "On Cold Damage"] and the *Jin gui yao lüe* [金櫃要略 "Essential Prescriptions of the Golden Coffer"].[146] Apart from being the work of a named, literati author, the *Shang han lun* became hugely influential in Chinese medicine because it was the first to combine the use of drug therapy with the theory of correspondences, and because it was one of the few works to focus on a single disease etiology. The "cold damage" of the title broadly indicates all externally contracted diseases, but narrowly refers to illnesses contracted through wind and cold.

The text was also influential because since the Song dynasty it has included a postface where Zhang states that he once had a family of over two hundred members, but most of these had died in a plague classified as "cold damage," which motivated him to study medicine. After indicating his desire to rescue suffering people, his postface concludes by citing Confucius's discussion of the levels of knowledge, and stating that his honoring the medical arts (*fang shu* 方術, literally "technical arts," as in the Lius' catalogue and the Yellow Emperor corpus) stems from following Confucius's words. As Miranda Brown has demonstrated, this postface only appears in Song editions, and the numerous earlier references to Zhang Ji never mention his loss of most of his kin. She argues that this effort to identify the author as a devoted Confucian literatus seeking to save the people reflects the emergence in the Song of the ideal of the "Confucian doctor" who combined literary cultivation with a career as a professional healer.[147] While this took place long after the period covered in this essay, it is plausible that the Song doctors embraced as their model the first individual to whom a medical text could be assigned, specifically the text that first systematically expounded the drug therapy that dominated Chinese medicine through the centuries.

[146] These were originally parts of a single work, the *Shang han za bing lun* (傷寒雜病論), which were re-organized by Wang Shuhe (210–285) in the Jin dynasty. The works currently circulating under these titles were largely assembled and commented from the Song dynasty onward.

[147] Brown, *The Art of Medicine in Early China*, ch. 5.

Conclusion: Therapies of the Self

Theories of cultivating a proper, embodied self emerged as a topic in East Asia in texts of the fourth century BCE, probably responding to the new political and social order of the Warring States, which demanded new ideals of personhood. Confucian texts elaborated theories of rituals that defined this new order, within which elite selves emerged through the roles in which they were embedded (and embodied). These rituals, whose overarching rubric was phonetically and graphically linked with the body, were also used to explain health or disease, and the attainment of full longevity or premature death. In the late Warring States, theoreticians of statecraft similarly theorized the state's subjects as relational persons defined in family units, legal codes, and the associated hierarchy of titles.

Warring States writers also theorized the embodied self as a product of *qi* energies that transferred substance between the person and the surrounding world. The most influential example was the poem "Inner Training" which traced out a process from correct bodily placement through mental cultivation to a perfect tranquility that opened the self to beneficent spirits, allowing mental powers to radiate outward to dominate other people, and ultimately the world. This process, which became enmeshed in the *Mencius*'s theory of the body as the ground of all virtues, thus provided the basis for a theory of rule through mastery of the embodied self. Virtually every text from the late Warring States, as well as early Han examples, articulated versions of this theory, often labelled "techniques of the heart/mind" and aiming to create a "sage" or "great man" who was both the ideal person and model ruler.

The late Warring States also witnessed other new theories or practices for cultivating the self. Thus, in Chu tombs from the fourth and third centuries, people who died violently or prematurely (a significant category in this age of large-scale war) were no longer turned into anonymous ancestors, but instead were guided by ritual specialists to become post-mortem selves who undertook a journey to a bureaucratic realm of the dead in the far northwest. This followed the increasing insistence that funerary rituals served to permanently separate the dead from the living. Scattered anecdotes and arguments also spoke of specialists in the arts of the kitchen or healing who shaped a healthy body that enabled the person to perform designated roles.

However, the most important accounts from this period of perfecting the embodied self were texts from Mawangdui and Zhangjiashan which describe hygienic techniques to improve health and extend longevity. The placement of these texts in tombs, and the nature of their contents, suggest that they circulated among educated members of the elite who were not physicians, but rather amateurs hoping to improve their own bodies and extend their lives. The techniques included guided breathing, physical exercises, sexual cultivation, and dietetics or herbal formulae, all focused on ingesting and circulating fresher *qi* energies. Only texts on channels and moxibustion (unlike in the later *Huangdi Neijing*, acupuncture is never mentioned) assume the work of a physician, and only one of these mentions students instructed by a master. At the same time, the account in the *Shi ji* of Chunyu Yi's healing practices shows how elite people received esoteric texts on diagnosing and treating the body. Excavated texts also demonstrate knowledge of healing by some officials and military officers, but there were no openly circulating works on medical theories.

Medicine was first established as an independent field of study with a defined body of publicly transmitted texts by Liu Xiang (and his son Liu Xin) at the end of the Western Han. In their catalogue of the imperial text collection, they identified medical texts as a subset of technical practices dealing with the body. This demonstrates the links between the creation of the imperial state and the definition of the arts for perfecting the embodied self as a technical, text-based discipline.

At the same time, and into the Eastern Han, unknown authors compiled a large corpus entitled the *Inner Classic of the Yellow Emperor*, which elaborated new theories of the body, disease, and therapy. These texts reveal the emergence of a community of literati and patrons who collected, disseminated, and employed the texts that figured in the bibliographic treatise. This new discourse on the body shifted away from multiple patient-centered curative traditions to a scientifically grounded, technical practice which privileged the theoretical knowledge of the physician, and thereby claimed superiority over the limited practices of earlier healers. These new-style healers, men of literary attainments who were the model "persons" of the new texts, asserted their authority over people who had previously developed and healed their own bodies, but were now reduced to the level of a patient whose body could be understood and healed only by the physician. This new text-based definition of technical medicine and the healer culminated at the end of the Han dynasty with the appearance of the first texts on medical theory by named authors. In this way, the interlinked redefinitions of medicine and of the cultivation of a superior self through philosophy and literature (as idealized by the late Han elite) became another element of the new honoring of textual composition (which had celebrated the writing of history, philosophy, poetry, and literary essays as the highest forms of life) and the associated transformation of the elite in the Eastern Han and following centuries.[148]

[148] Lewis, *Honor and Shame in Early China*, ch. 6.

Cambridge Elements

Ancient East Asia

Erica Fox Brindley
Pennsylvania State University

Erica Fox Brindley is Professor and Head in the Department of Asian Studies at Pennsylvania State University. She is the author of three books, co-editor of several volumes, and the recipient of the ACLS Ryskamp Fellowship and Humboldt Fellowship. Her research focuses on the history of the self, knowledge, music, and identity in ancient China, as well as on the history of the Yue/Viet cultures from southern China and Vietnam.

Rowan Kimon Flad
Harvard University

Rowan Kimon Flad is the John E. Hudson Professor of Archaeology in the Department of Anthropology at Harvard University. He has authored two books and over 50 articles, edited several volumes, and served as editor of Asian Perspectives. His archaeological research focuses on economic and ritual activity, interregional interaction, and technological and environmental change, in the late Neolithic and early Bronze Ages of the Sichuan Basin and the Upper Yellow River valley regions of China.

About the Series

Elements in Ancient East Asia contains multi-disciplinary contributions focusing on the history and culture of East Asia in ancient times. Its framework extends beyond anachronistic, nation-based conceptions of the past, following instead the contours of Asian sub-regions and their interconnections with each other. Within the series there are five thematic groups: 'Sources', which includes excavated texts and other new sources of data; 'Environments', exploring interaction zones of ancient East Asia and long-distance connections; 'Institutions', including the state and its military; 'People', including family, gender, class, and the individual and 'Ideas', concerning religion and philosophy, as well as the arts and sciences. The series presents the latest findings and strikingly new perspectives on the ancient world in East Asia.

Cambridge Elements

Ancient East Asia

Elements in the Series

Violence and the Rise of Centralized States in East Asia
Mark Edward Lewis

Bronze Age Maritime and Warrior Dynamics in Island East Asia
Mark Hudson

Medicine and Healing in Ancient East Asia: A View from Excavated Texts
Constance A. Cook

The Methods and Ethics of Researching Unprovenienced Artifacts from East Asia
Christopher J. Foster, Glenda Chao and Mercedes Valmisa

Environmental Foundations to the Rise of Early Civilisations in China
Yijie Zhuang

Self and Body in Early East Asian Thought
Mark Edward Lewis

A full series listing is available at: www.cambridge.org/EAEA

For EU product safety concerns, contact us at Calle de José Abascal, 56–1°, 28003 Madrid, Spain or eugpsr@cambridge.org.

www.ingramcontent.com/pod-product-compliance
Ingram Content Group UK Ltd.
Pitfield, Milton Keynes, MK11 3LW, UK
UKHW020409240726
473652UK00010B/484

* 9 7 8 1 1 0 8 9 7 2 1 9 2 *